ORAL HEALTH RELATED QUALITY OF LIFE – TRENDS IN ADOLESCENTS

DR ALI MOHAMMED MASHOOD

This is dedicated to my Family

Contents

Acknowledgements

Only with the Almighty's blessing that I have been able to complete this literary compilation. It is with utmost pleasure and immense gratitude that I acknowledge the enthusiastic and tireless participation of everyone who has helped me work on this library dissertation. Without their support and guidance, this endeavor would have remained a dream. I honor my Guide, Dr. REKHA R, with profound conviction and keen gratitude for her invaluable assistance and insightful suggestions that have contributed to the successful completion of this library dissertation. She has been positive and constructive, constantly driving me during the process of this project to aspire for excellence.

A heartfelt hat-tip to my colleagues, for their wholehearted support throughout my work. Most importantly, without the love and patience of my friends, Dr. Shruthika M & Dr. Somak S none of this would have been possible. All these years, my family has been a constant source of love, concern, support and strength. Words fail to express my love and respect for my family, Dr. Asifa Nisar, Dr. Mohammed Nisar Ali, Mubarrah Nisar, Muarrah Nisar, Hayaah Ibadullah, and Dr. Feroze Hussain who have stood by me through thick and thin, providing me with the strength and courage to face whatever has come by way.

ONE
INTRODUCTION

"The web of our life is of a mingled yarn—good and ill together." —Shakespeare, All's Well That Ends Well Oral health has been recognized as an important aspect of health, physical and mental well-being and quality of life. Oral health can be influenced by individual experiences, perceptions, values, expectations, adaptive strategies, behaviours, actions of people and communities.1

Quality of life is the individual perception about his/her expectations and position in life, context, values, and it is not properly measured by clinical health indicators alone.2 In turn, oral health-related quality of life (OHRQoL) measurements have been developed to address the limitation of these clinical indicators and to help informing the development of public health programs.3,4 The OHRQoL is a multidimensional construct that is related to the self-perception of an individual's oral health condition and that has also been widely used as an outcome evaluation of clinical treatments.2-5

Oral health-related quality of life (OHRQoL) comprises an apparently complex array of biological and psychological aspects of oral health. These measures of OHRQoL, however, have been criticized because they use mostly negative questions from theories and models to elicit responses to the presence of disease without considering the individual's ability to adapt or resist to such diseases.6,7 Also, they are limited for not including psychosocial characteristics (like the sense of coherence, self-esteem, psychological well-being) that seem to be important predictors of quality of life to all age groups including adolescents.8

Oral health is essential to the individual's overall health, contributing significantly to their OHRQoL. 4 During adolescence, social relations are established, characterized by the acceptance of individuals by the group. They are concerned with developing a style that appeals to themselves and their group of friends. 5–7 The involvement of anterior teeth by oral problems such as traumatic dental injuries (TDI) may exert a major influence on adolescents perceived oral health-related quality of life (OHRQoL).

This fact is due to physical discomfort, caused primarily by pain, and psychological problems such as difficulty in smiling, which may directly affect their social life. 8–10 There appear to be sex differences in OHRQoL, with some studies reporting poorer OHRQoL in females3,4,7, some reporting no sex differences8, and others reporting poorer OHRQoL among males, other factors being equal. 9 Ethnic differences have also been noted. 10

Low socioeconomic status, income, and education have all been shown to be associated with poorer OHRQoL in adolescents. 4,5,11,12 Caries experience has been reported in a number of studies to negatively affect OHRQoL. 8,13 This is not counter-intuitive: oral symptoms (such as pain or difficulty in chewing) would be expected to be more prevalent and severe in those with greater caries experience, and this would be reflected in poorer OHRQoL.

Where malocclusion is concerned, there have been consistent reports from adolescent population samples of a clear association between malocclusion severity and poor OHRQoL among adolescents. 8,16 Unlike that with caries, these associations were usually apparent with only the emotional and social well-being domains. 8,16,17 Adolescents with malocclusions have been shown to have a higher prevalence of self-reported oral problems, mainly affecting smiling, speaking, and eating. 18

The psychological well-being (PWB) of adolescents has shown to play a mediating role in OHRQoL. Children in the UK who were satisfied with their physical appearance reported fewer impacts on OHRQoL during the transition to secondary school3 . Children with better PWB are, in general, likely to report better OHRQoL regardless of their malocclusion or orthodontic treatment status6 . Individuals from lower socioeconomic position experience differential accumulation of negative exposures, lack of material resources and consequently, worse levels of health.

The psychosocial theory is based on the perceptions of the relative social status and how well people are able to cope with disease and poor health. 6, 8–10Psychosocial stress, low coping, and anxiety as a result of negative life events and lower social support are unequally distributed to the people from lower socioeconomic position and thus contribute to inequalities in oral health. 6, 10 Despite considerable research attention and effort in the last decade or so, much remains unclear about the biological, social, and psychological characteristics that impact on OHRQoL.

Because OHRQoL measures provide essential information when assessing the treatment needs of individuals and populations, for making clinical decisions, and when evaluating interventions, services, and programs, it is important to determine the relative contribution of these characteristics to OHRQoL to further clarify the possible role each has on OHRQoL

TWO

Introduction to Quality of Life

In the preamble of its constitution, the World Health Organization (WHO) states "Health is a state of complete physical, mental, and social well-being and not merely the absence of disease and infirmity." 19 Recent development in the definition of health and measurement of health status have little impact on dentistry. The dental profession has remained narrowly clinical in its approach to oral health equating health with disease. This is the reason why dentistry has remained immune to this broadening concept of health. So now it is important to know that quality of life (QOL) measures are not a substitute of measuring outcomes associated with the disease, but are adjunct to them.20 Oral health related quality of life (OHRQOL) is a relatively new, but rapidly growing phenomenon, which has emerged over the past 2 decades. Slade and others identified the shift in the perception of health from merely the absence of disease and infirmity to complete physical, mental, and social well-being, the definition of the WHO. This shift happened in the second half of the 20th century and it was the result organization (WHO) as the key issue in the conception of health-related quality of life (HRQOL) and subsequently OHRQOL a "silent revolution" in the values of highly industrialized societies from materialistic values that concentrate on economic stability and security to values focused on self-determination and self-actualization.21 OHRQOL as "a multidimensional construct that reflects (among other things) people's comfort when eating, sleeping, and engaging in social interaction; their self-esteem; and their satisfaction with respect to their oral health."22

Oral Health Related Quality of Life has become a priority for specialists as late as the 1980's, and then they focused on evaluating the consequences of oral disease on the life of the individual and the establishment of proper measures in order to cancel the negative effects of oral disease on the quality of life.23 The relation between the quality of life and oral health is defined as the evaluation, both from a personal and a medical point of view, of the way in which psychological, social factors and traumatizing and uncomfortable experiences affect an individual's well-being.24

According to child developmental psychology, children have the ability to make evaluative judgements of their appearance; the quality of friendships and other people's thoughts, emotions and behaviours gradually develops through middle childhood (6-10 years) and by the age of 11 or 12 they view health as a multidimensional concept organized around the following constructs: being functional, adhering to good lifestyle behaviours, a general sense of well-being and relationships with others. 25 OHRQOL is associated with Functional factors, Psychological factors, Social factors, and Experience of pain or discomfort.

Oral diseases seriously impair quality of life in a large number of individuals and they may affect various aspects of life, including function, appearance, interpersonal relationships and even career opportunities. 26 In turn, oral disease pattern is dependent on various socioeconomic characteristics of the children and parents. Behaviour and attitudes of children are formed and developed from social, cultural, economic and ethnic factors throughout their lives.

This process is also influenced by their knowledge of health and prevention of disease, including oral diseases.27 Parents gasp and clap in excitement as they witness their toddlers first steps or hear them babble their first words. Children's first day at school, their first piano recital, their first soccer game, can cause parents to beam with pride. However similar milestones during their children's transition into adulthood are much less welcome. This transitional period, from childhood to adulthood is called Adolescence and spans the ages of 12-19 years old. During adolescence the desire for independence and autonomy increase, and parents usually find themselves less thrilled with the developmental indicators of this increasing maturity.

Many adolescent people have ill habits that will have an impact n their oral health. In order to provide good oral health care, dental professionals must understand the complexities inherent to younger people, their special needs and their capacity to undergo and respond to care. Ideally the prevention of risk behaviours begins earlier in life but this stage of life brings such a cascade of events that even the most informed and well supported adolescent may find it difficult to adhere to practices recommended by care givers and institutions.

THREE

The Concept of Health and Quality of Life

This concept of health status embraces the biopsychosocial model of health into which symptoms, physical functioning, and emotional and social well-being are incorporated.28 Quality of life (QoL), or individuals' "perceptions of their position in life in the context of culture and value systems in which they live, and in relation to their goals, expectations, standards, and concerns"29 , is now recognized as a valid parameter in patient assessment in nearly every area of physical and mental healthcare, including oral health. Since Cohen and Jago (1976) first advocated the development of socio dental indicators, efforts have been invested in developing instruments to measure OHRQoL30,31,32 .

Further, the opportunity arose to consider how oral health affects aspects of social life, including self-esteem, social interaction, school and job performance, etc. Researchers began to postulate how oral health is related to health-related quality of life (HRQoL) and to understand the interrelationships between and among traditional clinical variables (like diagnosis), data from clinical examinations, and person-centred, self-reported health experience. The subjective evaluation of OHRQoL "reflects people's comfort when eating, sleeping and engaging in social interaction; their self-esteem; and their satisfaction with respect to their oral health"33. It is the result of an interaction between and among oral health conditions, social and contextual factors, and the rest of the body.

This model, adapted from Wilson and Cleary (1995), is built on psychological and social science theory and epidemiological findings. This framework links health status or clinical variables (e.g., type/extent of defect), functional status (e.g., speech), oral-facial appearance, psychological status, OHRQoL, and overall QoL. The model recognizes the effects of environmental or contextual factors (e.g., sociocultural factors, education, family structure) and access to care on oral health perceptions and related QoL.

Theoretically, OHRQoL is a function of various symptoms and experiences and represents the person's subjective perspective. With increasing focus of health policy to address health promotion and disease prevention, HRQoL and OHRQoL have come to incorporate both positive and negative perceptions of oral health and health outcomes 34 . Thus, assessments of oral health can reflect both negative impact and enhancement of self and well-being. For example, people may seek oral healthcare for preventive (e.g., cleanings) or elective (e.g., orthodontics) treatment. Health psychologists have recognized that psychological assets such as optimism and resilience correlate with an individual's QoL, particularly how well she or he is able to cope with disease and poor health. 35,36,37

This model incorporates positive psychology which has far-reaching implications in health delivery, since human strengths such as coping and social connectedness have been linked to better immunosuppressance, health outcomes, and mortality. Common dimensions in OHRQoL instruments are given in Fig. 3, along with specific examples of items associated with each dimension. While traditional factors like oral health symptoms are illustrated in this figure, factors such as social and emotional well-being incorporate positive health states such as happiness and confidence.

Recent OHRQoL instruments, like the Child Oral Health Impact Profile (COHIP), attempt to identify the impact of treatment (e.g., satisfaction) along with the "positive influence of oral health and the appearance of the face and teeth on overall health and well-being among patients and the nontreatment-seeking individuals" 34 Positive health attributes have also been incorporated into measures with youth, 38 adults, 39 and older persons. 40 In short, OHRQoL assesses positive and negative dimensions across the life course.

A number of authors have commented on the plethora of terms used in the literature on health and associated phenomena. 41 In addition, there is a tendency for key concepts, such as health status, health-related quality of life and quality of life to be used interchangeably with little consensus about what they mean and how they should be defined. 41 In the dental field, measures that draw on the patient's perspective were originally referred to as socio-dental indicators or measures of oral health status, subjective oral health or the social impacts of oral disease. Subsequently, these terms were replaced with the term OH-QoL, with measures being characterized as such irrespective of their content. This change in terminology is evident in the naming of measures.

While, the names of measures have changed, the type of items comprising the measures and the way in which they are scored has not. Some have argued that the notion of quality of life was adopted as it has a broader appeal than that of health status 42 and claim that most health-related quality of life measures used in medicine are in reality measures of functional status in a new guise.43

The relatively loose way in which terminology is used, and new labels applied to old endeavours, is also apparent in definitions of oral health and OH-QoL. For example, an early definition of oral health indicated that it was concerned with 'the functioning of the oral cavity and the person as a whole...and with subjectively perceived symptoms, such as pain and discomfort'. 44 A later definition offered by the same author was both more specific and more comprehensive: 'when talking about oral health, our focus is not on the oral cavity itself but on the individual and the way in which oral disorders, diseases and conditions threaten health, well-being and quality of life'. 45

In later contributions, OH-QoL was defined in relatively simple terms as 'the extent to which oral disorders affect functioning and psychosocial wellbeing' 46 and 'the symptoms and functional and psychosocial impacts that emanate. Oral health outcome measures developed to date 402, Locker & Allen diseases and disorders. 47 Kressin 48 defined OH-QoL in broad terms, as 'a broad conception of health, encompassing the traditional definition of health, as well as an individual's subjective impact of health on well-being and functioning in everyday life', and also more simply as 'the impact of oral conditions on daily functioning'.

Clearly, some of these definitions suggest that health-related quality of life equates with health, while others imply that it is something more than health, encompassing additional and broader dimensions of human experience. While there appears to be a consensus that disease, health and the quality of life are distinct concepts, as reflected in contemporary models of disease and its outcomes, exactly what is meant by health-related quality of life (and by extension OHQoL) has not been entirely resolved.

Consequently, 'whether the measures developed for use in oral research and practice should be considered to be indicators of health status or indicators of healthrelated quality of life is somewhat uncertain'. 47 The shift in nomenclature from 'oral health status' to 'oral health-related quality of life' appears to be based on the assumption that since measures address aspects of functioning that are compromised by oral diseases and disorders of various kinds, they must necessarily indicate how these diseases and disorders affect the quality of life.43 This is not the case; as Leplege and Hunt 43 suggest, the 'implications of measuring health status are quite different from those of measuring quality of life'.

Moreover, studies of those with chronic conditions have indicated that many report that their quality of life is good, in spite of quite severe physical limitations. 49 This 'disability paradox' suggests that health and quality of life are not only conceptually distinct but also empirically distinct. 50 There is also a compelling rationale for suggesting that measures of health status and measures of health-related quality of life are distinct. This view emerges out of the debate between Gill and Feinstein 51 and Guyatt and Cook 42 with respect to the appropriateness of patient-based outcome measurements in clinical trials.

Gill and Feinstein 51 , in their critical appraisal of the face validity of such measures, identified a number of criteria that must be met if a measure is to be used to assess what they call 'quality of life', but which Guyatt and Cook 42 more properly characterize as 'health related quality of life'. Relatively, few of the studies examined by Gil and Feinstein 51 that claimed to measure quality of life met these criteria. Guyatt and Cook 42 believe that these criteria are too stringent and offer a more limited set by means of which measures may be evaluated.

FOUR

MEASURES OF OHRQoL

Medicine in the last 30 years has seen the increasing use of the terms 'health-related quality of life' and 'quality of life' in relation to the outcomes of health conditions and therapy for those conditions. 52 This emerged out of a growing recognition that traditional clinical measures of health need to be supplemented by data obtained from patients and or persons that captures their experiences and concerns. 53 It reflects the fact that we are no longer aiming just to prolong life or to render it free of disease, but to make it better. 54

It also acknowledges that the issues addressed by the term's health-related quality of life and quality of life are important determinants of care seeking, adherence to treatment regimens and satisfaction with the care received. 55 Consequently, there has been a tremendous growth in the literature concerned with these constructs. This is also the case in dentistry, where there has been a proliferation of instruments and scales seeking to assess what has come to be called oral health-related quality of life (OHRQoL) and or the quality of life of patients with various oral conditions. Ten such measures were described in a monograph reporting the proceedings of a major conference on measuring oral health and quality of life. 56

Since then, at least six additional measures have been developed and more are in the process of development. However, the development of so many measures, to be welcomed when the field was in its infancy, has led to a certain lassitude and a failure to continue to address the conceptual and methodological issues involved in measuring perceptions of oral health and the outcomes of oral disorders at the individual and population levels. The existence of numerous measures which appear to be appropriate for a wide variety of contexts and purposes seems to have given rise to the assumption that these theoretical and measurement problems have been satisfactorily addressed and or solved.

This is not the case in medicine where critical reviews of the state of the art continue to appear that question the theoretical basis of measures that claim to assess health-related quality of life or quality of life. 52–55, 57 In contrast, while the monograph referenced above 56 contained comprehensive descriptions of the first oral disease specific measures to be developed, the descriptions were largely concerned with their content, scoring methods and technical properties rather than with the more fundamental question of what a measure actually measures and the values on which it is based. 58

Although the issue of what is being measured would seem to be encompassed by the notion of construct validity, the fact that scores derived from a measure discriminate between the dentate and the edentulous or that they show associations with global ratings of oral health, tells us little about the underlying construct being addressed. Similarly, the fact that scores change in the expected direction after a therapeutic intervention tell us only that change has occurred; change scores do not, in and of themselves, indicate exactly what it is that has changed.

This is primarily a conceptual and methodological issue linked to how the attribute being measured is defined and how a measure of that attribute was developed. Despite the fact that there are differences between the two approaches, both imply that two broad and overlapping questions need to be considered when evaluating a measure in terms of the underlying construct being assessed: First, is the measure patient- or person-centred, and second, does it incorporate aspects of daily life that are important to patients or persons which may be compromised by disorders of various kinds?

The importance of patient or person centring Despite considerable disagreement over definitions there is an emerging consensus that measures addressing overall or components of quality of life should reflect the perspectives of patients and or the lay public. 55, 60, 61 Measures that meet this criterion are patient or person-centred rather than expert-centred. 55, 61 Many measures that claim to assess health related quality of life or quality of life have been criticized because they reflect the values and concerns of physicians, social scientists or other experts rather than patients or persons and what they consider to be relevant. 55, 59, 62 Leplege and Hunt 55 have gone so far as to claim that 'there has been some confusion between questionnaires that are completed by patients and those that reflect the concerns of the patients.

Too often patients are asked to complete questionnaires that do not reflect their concerns'. The main mechanism by means of which patient or lay perspectives can be accommodated is through the use of qualitative interviews. According to Guyatt et al. 63,64 , the items comprising questionnaires that claim to capture quality of life issues must be derived from in-depth interviews with those who will ultimately be expected to complete the questionnaire.

Consequently, one way of evaluating OH-QoL measures is the way in which the items comprising the measure where developed. Were they derived from qualitative interviews with the target population? If not, and since items may legitimately be obtained from other sources such as literature reviews or clinical opinion, 64 is there any evidence from these other sources or elsewhere that the items do fully address the concerns of those who will be expected to complete the questionnaire? That is, did the investigators achieve content coverage, a component of content validity that is as important as criterion validity but most often neglected?

Establishing importance The discussion so far implies that the main distinction between a measure of oral health status and a measure of OH-QoL is a simple one. As Gill and Feinstein 52 state: 'The need to incorporate patient's values and preferences is what distinguishes quality of life from all other measures of health'. That is, do the items comprising the questionnaire refer to aspects of daily life that are important to the target population?

How can importance be established? Although qualitative studies are a first step in eliciting the views of patients and persons regarding what is important, they are insufficient in and of themselves. The reason for this is that while qualitative interviews can reveal what is salient to the interviewees, the interview may reveal a range of experiences some of which are relatively more and some relatively less important. Moreover, if the questionnaire is to be used in clinical trials or other studies where the unit of analysis is the group, some way has to be found of identifying which experiences are of most importance on average to the group who will be participating in the study.

The solution proposed by Guyatt et al. 64 is an item impact study. Here items derived from qualitative interviews are given to a group of patients or persons who indicate if they experience the problem described by the item and, if so, how much bother or distress it causes. Item impact scores are calculated by multiplying the prevalence of the problem by its mean bother rating, items ranked according to these scores and the top ranking items selected for the final questionnaire. The limitation of this approach is that a high prevalence and low impact item may be more highly scored than a low prevalence high impact item, so that items of importance to a minority of patients or people may not make it into the final questionnaire.

Consequently, the item-impact approach produces a group-centred rather than a patient-centred questionnaire. 65 This much is recognized by Guyatt and Cook. 54 While group centred questionnaires may be appropriate for clinical trials, they concede that they may not be appropriate for clinical practice. When clinicians are making treatment decisions, they should consider an individual patient's values since these may differ from or be masked by the aggregated values of those participating in an item impact study.

This points to the fact that 'quality of life – even when health-related – has different components, significance and meaning that are unique to the individual'. 65 In fact, the main 'challenge to measuring quality of life lies in its uniqueness to individuals'. 59 A solution to this dilemma is to be found in the recommendations of Gill and Feinstein 52 for improving the measurement of health-related quality of life.

These are: rate frequency, severity and importance; allow respondents to add supplemental items, and use global ratings which are summary variables and can reflect the differing values and preferences of a group of individuals. This means that a questionnaire must have a complex structure – questions that document experiences; importance ratings that indicate the value an individual attaches to those experiences; open-ended questions to elicit experiences not covered by the questionnaire, and global ratings of quality of life and health-related quality of life. If these requirements are not met a measure is not addressing health-related quality of life; rather it is a measure of health status. Carr et al. 59, make essentially the same point in arguing for the use of individualized measures. These measures allow respondents to select issues and concerns that are affected by health rather than providing a standardized predetermined list. 53

However, they acknowledge that the completion of such questionnaires is time consuming and difficult. Moreover, the aggregation, analysis and interpretation of the data are challenging, particularly with respect to group comparisons and change over time. This raises the interesting question of whether or not we can legitimately refer to the quality of life of a group and, if so, how quality of life might be measured at the group level.

Evaluating measures of 'oral health-related quality of life' Although the arguments concerning the individualized nature of quality of life and health-related quality of life are compelling, we tend to agree with Guyatt and Cook 54 and find the criteria of Gill and Feinstein 52 somewhat demanding. Accordingly, when evaluating so-called measures of 'oral health-related quality of life', particularly with respect to what they measure, we devised a set of criteria more akin to those of Guyat and Cook 54 than Gill and Feinstein. 52 These were:

1. Is the stated aim to measure health-related quality of life or quality of life and is this explicit? If so, are these constructs defined and their constituent domains identified?

2. If not, is an alternative construct measured by the instrument specified and defined and its constituent domains identified?

3. Do the investigators specify the contexts in which the measure is to be used? Was it developed to be used with groups (as in surveys or clinical trials) or individuals (as in clinical practice)?

4. Were the items comprising the questionnaire derived from qualitative interviews with those who will be completing the questionnaire?

5. Is there evidence that the aspects of life the items address are important to those who will be completing the questionnaire?

6. Does the questionnaire contain global ratings of health-related quality of life or quality of life?

7. How was the measure validated? Was it tested against oral health indicators or were broader indicators that may capture aspects of quality of life used? In order to illustrate the application of these criteria, we reviewed the four mostly widely used measures of the outcomes of oral disorders; namely, the Geriatric Oral Health Assessment Index, 66 the Oral Health Impact Profile (OHIP), 67 the Oral Impacts on Daily Performances (OIDP) 68 and the Child Oral Health Quality of Life Questionnaires. 69 In addition, we also review the Oral Health Quality of Life Inventory. 70

Although not widely used, this measure has some distinct features which make it of interest from a conceptual point of view. The 'data' were the initial papers describing the development and psychometric evaluation of these measures. Where such papers were not available, the summaries presented in the monograph of papers from the 1997 conference 67 were used.

FIVE

INSTRUMENTS & OHRQoL

The oral health-related quality of life (OHRQoL) concept refers to self-reports specifically pertaining to oral health, and captures both the functional, social and psychological impacts of oral disease. 71 Shifting the purpose of measurement from disease conditions to the perceived impacts of oral diseases, the measures have varied from direct clinically based indices indicating normative needs to indirect measures of felt need in terms of self-report indicators.

The measures have varied from instruments to measure single dimensions of oral health to scoring systems comprising composite socio-dental indicators or OHRQoL measures. Socio-dental indicators are defined as any measure to estimate the social impact of oral conditions 72 or the extent to which dental and oral conditions disrupt an individual's quality of life.

The various OHRQoL indicators are to varying extent based on a conceptual framework derived from the International Classification of Impairments, Disabilities and Handicaps (ICIDH) developed by WHO in 1980, 73 and that was subsequently amended for dentistry by Locker. 74 The ICIDH model consists of the following key concepts: impairments, functional limitations, pain, disability and handicap. It provides a theoretical basis for the empirical exploration of the links between various dimensions of health and oral health. Clinical studies using patient-based outcome measures have shown that they can provide new information about the effectiveness of different treatments, 75 and such measures are now generally accepted as the ultimate outcome of the oral health care system. 76 The concept of OHRQoL has been confirmed and validated cross-culturally by the ICSII study (Comparing Oral Health Care Systems, a second international collaborative study) in the context of a multinational investigation of oral health determinants and outcomes. 77

A first step in selecting an appropriate OHRQoL instrument is to specify the exact purpose or aim in using such a measure in terms of being descriptive, discriminative or evaluative. The second step is to identify a measure whose properties conform to the intended study aims. In some cases, there will be need for generic instruments and in other cases for more condition specific measurements. Instruments used in survey research will need specific qualities, while the use of questionnaires in longitudinal designs intended to measure change in OHRQoL on population- or on individual levels represents greater methodological challenges. 78

It cannot be assumed that a measure proved to be reliable and valid in cross-sectional population studies will be suitable for the purpose of detecting meaningful clinical changes in a longitudinal intervention. The latter purpose needs properties such as responsiveness and interpretability. 79 To date, the responsiveness of many OHRQoL instruments has not been established, although there is an increasing tendency to use OHRQoL measures as outcomes in clinical trials and evaluation studies. Longitudinal studies assessing changes in OHRQoL as a time effect or in response to treatment and preventive procedures are needed, 80 to explore those qualities. 81

For oral health related quality of life measurements, many different instruments already exist. While most of the measures appear to be theory based and well tested for psychometric properties, only a few of them have been widely used by others in addition to the ones responsible for their development. There is need for an assessment aimed at presenting a priority of recommended instruments to be used for different purposes, and then plan for future research for further evaluations. The first step in this process should be to explore and evaluate existing instruments.

Oral Health Impact Profile The original OHIP-instrument (OHIP-49) (49 items) was developed by Slade and Spencer 82 based on a conceptual framework of oral disease and its functional and psychological consequences. The instrument is divided into seven subscales (functional limitations, pain, psychological discomfort, physical disability, psychological disability, social disability and disadvantage). 82,83 This instrument is widely used and tested, also in longitudinal studies to evaluate change in quality of life among elderly people and in patients with implant retained dentures. 84,85 Shortened versions of the original scale have been developed, providing somewhat compromised instruments in terms of content validity.

The OHIP-14 version is a shortened version of the original OHIP-49- item scale. 82 It is easy to use, and has been tested for psychometric qualities in several studies in different populations (Figure 4). The OHIP14 has been shown to have measurement properties comparable with the full 49- item version. 86 The short version instrument has also been used in clinical trials 87 and shown to be sensitive to clinical effects of treatment. 88 The fully developed instrument (49 items) has, however, been shown to be better with respect to responsiveness than the shorter versions. 89 We are suggesting that both the Oral Health Impact Profile (OHIP-49) and the shortened version Oral Health Impact Profile (OHIP-14) could be included in the core group of instruments. They have both been tested extensively and shown to have good construct, discriminative and longitudinal validity.

The Oral Health Impact Profile (OHIP-EDENT) is also a modified shortened (20 items) version of the original 49-item scale. This modified version has been shown to have measurement properties comparable with the full 49-item version 86 and may be more appropriate for use in edentulous patients than the short version OHIP-14. We suggest that the (OHIP-EDENT) could be included as one of the Group 2 instruments (Figure 5). The OHIP 105 was based on the ICIDH model of disease and its consequences. It intends to assess the 'social impact' of oral disorders, that is, the dysfunction, discomfort and disability caused by these conditions.

The purpose of the measure is broad; assessing priorities of care by documenting social impact among individuals and groups, understanding oral health behaviours, evaluating dental treatment and providing information for advocating for oral health. As such the intention was to develop a measure of self-perceived oral health. In developing the measure, an initial set of 535 statements were obtained from open-ended interviews with 64 dental patients recruited from private practices and dental hospital clinics. This item pool was reduced to a set of 46 unique statements based on their form and content and ability to represent one of six domains derived from the conceptual model.

Three additional statements representing the concept of handicap were taken from an existing generic health status measure. 106 While the qualitative component of the development process suggests that the OHIP is patient-centred, the item reduction process was expert-centred, designed to select items according to their fit with a conceptual framework rather than on the basis of their importance to the patients from whom they were derived. Why some statements were retained and others discarded is not described. Severity weights for each of the statements, designed to reflect their relative importance, were provided, but these were based on the judgments of a panel comprised of members of community groups, dental practitioners and students. Consequently,the weights may not reflect the severity and/or importance of the events described by the items as perceived by individual dental patients or dental patients as a group. 107

The OHIP was initially validated by demonstrating an association between scale and sub-scale scores and perceived need to visit a dentist. Further validation of the OHIP as a measure of oral health status has been provided by numerous investigators; scores distinguish between the dentate and edentulous and show small to moderate correlations with a wide range of traditional clinical indicators and self-perceived oral conditions, such as xerostomia. Some evidence that the events captured by the OHIP may be of broader significance than oral health has been provided by the study of the institutionalized elderly referenced above. 108

These indicated that OHIP scores were significantly associated with life satisfaction and, unlike the Geriatric Oral Health Assessment Index (GOHAI), the association remained clearly significant after controlling for other predictors. This suggests that what could be regarded as an expert-centred measure of subjective oral health may be capturing events which impact on general well-being and quality of life. However, the items comprising the measure do not in and of themselves demonstrate that this is the case. UK Oral Health-Related Quality of Life Measure (OHQoL-UK)

This instrument is also widely tested and used in different studies, both cross-sectional and longitudinal design. The instrument is easy to use, has shown good psychometric qualities and also found to be sensitive to clinical effects of treatment. 90 We are suggesting that the instrument could be included in the core group. Oral Impacts on Daily Performances (OIDP) This instrument has 8 (9) items comprising one domain (the ultimate impacts or physical, psychological and social aspects of performance of daily living) and satisfactory psychometric qualities in terms of reliability (internal consistency and test-retest) crosssectional construct and discriminative validity have been established in different cultural contexts. 91,92,93,94,95,96,97 The OIDP is a distinctive measure in many respects.

First, it is one of the few that was developed with a very explicit purpose in mind; that is, to be used in conjunction with normative measures to assess population dental needs in order to facilitate dental service planning. 109 Second, it measures what are referred to as the 'ultimate' i.e. behavioural impacts of oral disorders and the extent to which the ability to perform physical, psychological and social performances is compromised. It is based on a modified version of the ICIDH model so that the physical, psychological and social issues it addresses are intended to be equivalent to 'the disability and handicap dimensions' of the model. Perhaps, because it was developed in the early 1990s, descriptions of the development of the OIDP do not include terms, such as health-related quality of life or quality of life. However, the children's version of the measure, developed in 2004 110 is described as a measure of OH-QoL. The OIDP originally consisted of nine items selected from the Comparison Table of Disability Indices and other general and oral health status measures.

The rationale for selecting the nine items originally comprising the OIDP is not provided so it is uncertain whether the measure achieves content validity. Moreover, since no patients or lay persons appear to have been involved in the selection of the activities to be addressed by the measure the OIDP appears to be the most expert centred of the measures reviewed. However, the OIDP is distinct in that it employs a more complex item scoring system than most measures and assesses both frequency and severity of impacts. The item severity score indicates how much trouble the event described by the item caused to their daily living. Assuming that severity can be equated with importance, this item self-weighting approach means that the measure goes some way towards meeting the importance criterion as defined above.

The instrument consists of eight items covering physical, psychological and social performances (eating and enjoying food, speaking and pronouncing clearly, cleaning teeth, sleeping and relaxing, smiling, laughing and showing teeth without embarrassment, maintaining usual emotional state without being irritable, carrying out major work or social role, and enjoying contact with people). 91 The scale assesses the frequency and the severity of the impact. The scores are weighted for each item and then summed to a total OIDP score. It is easy to apply in large population studies being short and in evaluating the ultimate outcomes of oral diseases.

It is also easier to assess psychometric properties of behaviours compared to concepts like feelings, evaluations etc (measures reflect underlying phenomena). Recent research indicates that the instrument is responsive to change, 98 and we find this instrument so promising that it is proposed as one of the core group instruments. Geriatric (General) Oral Health Assessment Index (GOHAI) This instrument was developed and tested by Atchison and Dolan (1990) 99 for evaluating functional status, pain and discomfort, worry, ability to chew and swallow, and social functioning. The initial testing showed satisfactory psychometric properties, but correlated only weekly with some of the oral status indexes. The scale has been widely used, and also tested longitudinally for changes in perceived oral health among elderly. 100,101 The instrument is age specific and could be one of the Group 2 instruments (Figure 5)

The GOHAI is a 12-item measure of 'patient reported oral functional problems' and 'psychosocial impacts associated with oral diseases' intended for use in the assessment of the effectiveness of dental treatment. 111 It is unclear whether this means it is intended for use in clinical practice with individual patients, or, with groups of patients in clinical trial settings. The overall construct being assessed by the GOHAI is not specified though it is 'based on a patient-centred definition of oral health'. Its 12 items were derived from an initial pool of 36 items developed following a literature review, consultations with health care providers and qualitative interviews with people attending seniors' centres and dental clinics.

Considering the item selection, the rationale for selecting the final 12 items and excluding the remaining 24 items is not apparent. However, items were chosen to reflect three distinct hypothesized dimensions, namely Measures of oral health-related quality of life physical function, psychosocial function and, pain and discomfort. Accordingly, the item selection process appears to have followed an expert rather than patient- or person-centred approach. Although the items selected address issues that are likely to be important, the authors provide no evidence that this is the case. Given that there are only 12 items, it is likely that the concerns of some patients will not be captured by this measure. This is recognized by the authors when they suggest that the measure could be expanded to 'reflect more of the elements of quality of life'. 111

Initial validation of the measure was based on the association of GOHAI scores and clinical measures of oral health status. A study of an institutionalized elderly population took a broader approach and reported a significant but weak correlation between GOHAI scores and a life satisfaction scale, although the association barely reached significance when controlling for other predictors of life satisfaction. 108 Consequently, the measure meets few of the criteria required of a measure of health-related quality of life.

As its title suggests, the GOHAI is best regarded as a measure of subjective oral health status. Child oral health related quality of life questionnaires The Child Oral Health Quality of Life Questionnaire (COHQOL) has been designed to assess the impact of oral and orofacial conditions on the quality of life of children and their families. 102 The Family Impact Scale is one component of the COHQOL and consists of Child Perception Questionnaires (CPQ 11-14 and CPQ 6-10) and the Parental-Caregiver Perceptions Questionnaire (P-CPQ).

Dependent on the age of the children, child oral health-related quality of life has to be measured either based on the caregiver's or the child's own views. Studies have indicated that both the views of the caregiver (measured by PPQ) and of the child itself (CPQ 11-14) should be included to fully represent child oral health-related quality of life. 103 This child oral health related quality of life questionnaires could be included in the expanded level of instruments group as a supplement to the core group instruments.

The Child Oral Health Quality of Life Questionnaire is a battery of measures for children and their parents (112, 113-115). Since all were developed using a similar process, this review is limited to the Child Perceptions Questionnaire for those aged 11–14 years (CPQ11- 14). 112 The aim was to produce a measure applicable to children with a wide range of dental, oral and oro-facial disorders, which conformed to contemporary concepts of child health.

Since the instrument was intended for use as an outcome measure in clinical trials and evaluation studies it needed to have properties suitable for the assessment of change at the group level. The instrument was developed to measure 'the oral health-related quality of life of children'. OH-QoL was not specifically defined, although the authors do indicate that measures of this construct 'document the functional and psychosocial outcomes of oral disorders. Items for the measure were developed by a two-stage process.

First, a preliminary item pool was developed by a review of existing oral health and child health status measures. Second, the relevance, clarity and comprehensiveness of these items were assessed in a face and content validity study by an expert panel composed of health professionals who treat children with oral and oro-facial disorders and parents of child patients with these conditions. Based on their comments, a modified item pool was developed which was revised further following in-depth interviews with a small number of child patients. Items for the final questionnaire were selected using an item impact study. As described above, this identifies those items of most importance to the patient population who will be asked to complete the questionnaire.

Consequently, the measure meets one of the criteria for a patient or person-centred scale. However, since the qualitative component of the study and the extent to which the child patients contributed to the items comprising the questionnaire is not described, it does not meet all those requirements. Orthognathic Quality of Life Questionnaire The OQoLQ is a condition-specific instrument for patients with severe dento-facial deformities requiring orthognathic treatment. 104 We suggest that such condition specific instruments should be included in the expanded level of instruments group. Parental-Caregiver Perceptions Questionnaire — P-CPQ and Family Impact Scale — FIS The P-CPQ has 31 items distributed into 4 subscales: 6 oral symptoms (OS), 8 functional limitations (FL), 7 emotional wellbeing (EWB) and 10 social wellbeing (SWB).

The questions refer only to the frequency of events in the previous 3 months. The items have 5 Likert response options: 'never=0', 'once or twice=1', 'sometimes=2', 'often=3', 'every day or almost every day=4'. A 'don't know' response also was permitted and scored as 0. Global ratings of the child's oral health and impact of the oral condition on his or her overall wellbeing were obtained from the parents/caregivers. The global ratings had a 5-point response format from 'excellent=0' to 'poor=4' for oral health and 'not at all=0' to 'very much=4' for wellbeing. The P-CPQ score is calculated by summing the response codes to all 31 items and dividing this sum by the number of items for which a valid response is obtained. The P-CPQ was developed for use with younger children and provides a measure of a child's OHRQoL. Where both parental and child reports are used, the P-CPQ can be regarded as complementing the latter, thus providing a comprehensive profile of a child's health and well-being.

The FIS is included in the P-CPQ and consists of 14 items that attempted to capture the effect of a child's oral or oro-facial condition on four domains: related to parental and family activities with 5 questions, parental emotions (4 questions), family conflict (4 questions) and family finances (1 question). The questions ask about the frequency of events in the previous 3 months. Response options for the four domains and the respective scores were: 'Never' (scoring 0); 'Once or twice' (1); 'Sometimes' (2); 'Often' (3); and 'Everyday' or 'Almost every day' (4). A 'Don't know' (DK) response was also allowed. The FIS scores are computed by summing all of the item scores. Scores for each of the four domains can also be computed. The final score could vary from 0 to 56, for which a higher score denoted a greater degree of the impact of child's oral conditions on the functioning of parents-caregivers and the family as a whole. In 2013 Thomson and Cols developed the short form of the P-CPQ 116 obtaining a 16-and 8- item short-form versions of the P-CPQ and FIS-8 short forms that were developed using data from two New Zealand pre/post-test interventional studies. The internal reliability, validity and responsiveness of the short-form versions were acceptable.

Directions for future research No single instrument can be regarded as a standard, comprehensive instrument for measurement of OHRQoL. There will always be a need for generic and more diseases/condition specific instruments. Characteristics of a good instrument may differ for group comparisons for public health purposes compared to measurement of within-subject changes.

The present evaluation clearly shows that there is need for more research to be able to recommend a final list of core instruments that should be used in different types of research exploring OHRQoL aspects. A lot of methodological issues are still not finally evaluated for the assessment of quality-of-life aspects. Future studies should be designed to test the instruments' discriminating qualities for different kinds of interventions in different age groups and populations. The present list should be regarded as preliminary and as a basis for the selection of instruments for future studies.

SIX

FACTORS AFFECTING OHRQOL

Oral health-related quality of life (OHRQoL) as a multidimensional concept is affected by many factors. OHRQoL measures not only oral symptoms and functional limitations, but also their impacts on patients' psychosocial status. Psychosocial status is liable to change according to age; hence the quality of life is a "dynamic construct" that is likely to change over time.117

Different models have been used to support the social determinants of health, among which the model proposed by Victora et al. 118 employs hierarchical frameworks to investigate the determinants of diseases by using multivariate analysis techniques. Health Related Quality of Life (HRQoL) is an important subjective component so it will depend on the relationship that each individual has with his life. This concept will vary and depend largely on the perception that people have about their physical, mental, social, and spiritual state, largely depending on their values, convictions, and beliefs, as well as their personal cultural context and history. 119

Clinicians interested in knowing the effects of interventions or treatments also find useful information on HRQoL, as it evaluates the final result of medical interventions at one point, not only assessing according to biological or physiological standards but also at an emotional, social, and functional level evaluating everything a person represents. Similarly, this information is also relevant to patients and family members making them aware of areas where their performance is affected by their health, identifying where they may need further help or therapy, or supporting them to choose between various options of treatments.

Moreover, it has been identified that the assessment of HRQoL in children can be used as a predictor of costs in health care and can help to identify risk groups or to evaluate health services. 120,121 Keeping in mind, OHRQoL deals with conditions that vary in intensity and relevance, making some life-threatening (oral cancers) some chronic (caries, periodontitis, etc.) some dealing with aesthetics (fluorosis, dental anomalies, etc), and rest related to oral pain (pulpitis, dental treatments, etc.). Oral health-related quality of life (OHRQoL) comprises an apparently complex array of biological and psychological aspects of oral health. For example, according to the Wilson and Cleary model, the health-related quality of life experienced by a person is not only determined by the nature and severity of the disorder or disease, but also by his/her characteristics and environment. 122

Furthermore, Quality of Life is by itself multi-faceted, showing the variation over time for each individual. 123 Along the time several oral conditions have been reported in the literature as conditions having an impact on OHRQoL. An example is edentulism, a condition that can affect masticatory function, dietary choice, and nutritional level. It has been reported that wearing dentures may interfere with the ability to eat satisfactorily, talk clearly and laugh freely. Tooth loss is one of the worst types of damage to oral health, causing aesthetic and functional problems. In addition to biological causes of tooth loss, socioeconomic factors contribute to oral health associated with tooth loss. Socioeconomic status is related to inequalities in health, and socioeconomically disadvantaged people have higher risks of disease and suffer more from health conditions. 124 Several studies have reported an association between tooth loss and OHRQoL.

Some other common oral conditions, such as caries, periodontal disease, which are almost universal in prevalence, and which are chronic but with acute recurring episodes, also impact on QoL. Similarly, other conditions that might not be as common as the ones mentioned before but which prevalence cannot be considered low as dental fluorosis, craniofacial disorders and oral cancer could be life-threatening. Several reports exhibit dental caries creating a negative impact on OHRQoL in populations of various ages across the globe, in children 125 and adults.

Especially, children with caries whose scores can be about 50% greater than scores for children without caries. 126 Among toddlers and preschool-age early childhood caries (ECC) is one of the most common health problems among children with periodontal disease have lower OHRQoL compared with the general population. Studies investigated the contextual socioeconomic effects of OHRQoL in adolescents. However, the majority of the studies assessed the effect of clinical oral conditions on OHRQoL adjusted for contextual socioeconomic factors. Adolescents attending a poor school environment characterized by lack of security and bullying at school had a greater likelihood of a poor OHRQoL. 127 The findings demonstrated that the mean income of the school's neighborhood was associated with higher overall CPQ11-14 scores overtime. It has been hypothesized that the environment may influence adolescents' behavior and their perception of oral health. 127

Another alteration that affects the quality of life is malocclusion. Authors as Onyeaso and Aderinokun in 2003, who conducted a study involving 614 Nigerian children aged 12-18 years, found a correlation between the malocclusion severity and the perception that children have about their dental appearance. There is an association seen between the presence of malocclusion and OHRQoL. Particularly the one related to lack of space in between teeth, facial pain has adverse effects on body image, social interaction, and daily behavior of an individual.

Not just the malocclusion but also its treatment has an effect on OHRQoL consequently affecting their functions and aesthetics. For instance, reports have been made demonstrating striking changes in self-concept and emotional health after orthodontic and surgical treatment of malocclusions and orofacial defects. Another alteration that has an impact on OHRQoL is severe hypodontia. It was associated with worse quality of life. Wong and Cols. observed that 100% of children reported having an impact in the area of oral symptoms, functional limitations in 88%, 55% to 100% emotional and social welfare. The number of missing teeth was associated moderately with the level of impact.

One of the main impacts of OHQRL noted in literature was the difficulty chewing, especially among the elderly. In Uganda, a study aiming to describe the OHRQoL in 12 years of age rural children showed that more than half of them reported oral impact "often" or "every day". Authors concluded that the presence of caries experience or treatment was associated with higher impacts on quality of life. The socially significant fluorosis was associated with a greater number of impacts, but not with higher total scores. Despite low levels of oral problems, these children experienced impacts on quality of life due to oral problems.

Finding that most responsible for these impacts is the presence of caries and fluorosis at a lower level. Also, craniofacial disorders cause an impact on OHRQoL including limitations in verbal and nonverbal communication, social interaction, and intimacy. Individuals with facial disfigurements due to craniofacial diseases and conditions and their treatments may experience loss of self-image and self-esteem, anxiety, depression, and social stigma; these, in turn, may limit educational, career, and marital opportunities and affect other social relations. Diet, nutrition, sleep, psychological status, social interaction, school, and work are affected by impaired oral and craniofacial health. Documented data, reported in Thailand, suggests that 90% of pre-adolescents have an impact related to the oral health of which 46% reported their emotional stability was affected. 128 Andiappan and cols. performed a meta-analysis and revealed that those receiving treatment for malocclusion and in individuals without malocclusion have significantly better OHRQoL compared to those with such condition.129

Besides clinical conditions, other factors that contributed to the impact on OHRQoL as lower family income and sex. In general, women reported a greater impact on OHRQoL than men, although no differences are observed between clinical conditions present in each gender. Differences in the perception of OHRQoL between the genders may be caused by individual and subjective concepts related to beauty and personal aesthetic standards, imposed by social demands and personal needs. 130

Socioeconomic inequalities are recognized as a major problem with people in low socioeconomic groups having worse subjective oral health outcomes, including oral health-related quality of life (OHRQoL). However, only a few longitudinal studies assessed the impact of contextual and individual socioeconomic determinants in adolescents' OHRQoL. Adolescents from low socioeconomic backgrounds reported worse OHRQoL at 2-year follow-up compared to those from the high socioeconomic background.

Actions toward health inequalities need to address socioeconomic factors in adolescence.131 A cross-sectional study conducted by Ling Sun et al. aimed to analyze the sociodemographic and clinical factors that may influence the OHRQoL of adolescents stated that gender was not a significant factor of OHRQoL whereas household income affected OHRQoL more than parents' education did: household income had effects on physical pain, psychological discomfort, psychological disability, and the total OHIP. As for clinical factors, unhealthy periodontal conditions were more prevalent than caries (94.67% vs. 59.00%); however, both of them showed no effect on OHRQoL.

Malocclusion had a negative effect on OHRQoL; the most affected subscales were psychological discomfort and psychological disability.132 The study conducted by Burak Buldur & Ozge Nur Güvendi revealed a valid demonstrable path of association between parental socioeconomic status, dental anxiety, childhood dental anxiety, oral health behaviors, and OHRQoL.133

SEVEN

ADOLESCENTS

1. Definition: Adolescence, transitional phase of growth and development between childhood and adulthood. The World Health Organization (WHO) defines an adolescent as any person between ages 10 and 19. This age range falls within WHO's definition of young people, which refers to individuals between ages 10 and 24. Adolescence has been described as the period in life when an individual is no longer a child, but not yet an adult. It is a period in which an individual undergoes enormous physical and psychological changes. Besides, the adolescent experiences change in social expectations and perceptions. Physical growth and development are accompanied by sexual maturation, often leading to intimate relationships. The individual's capacity for abstract and critical thought also develops, along with a sense of self-awareness when social expectations require emotional maturity. 134

2. **Age groups:** WHO defines adolescents as individuals in the 10-19-year age group and "youth" as the 15-24- year age group. These two overlapping age groups are combined in the group "young people", covering the age range 10-24 years. 135 WHO clearly recognizes that "adolescence" is a phase rather than a fixed time period in an individual's life. As indicated above, it is a phase of development on many fronts: from the appearance of secondary sex characteristics (puberty) to sexual and reproductive maturity; the development of mental processes and adult identity; and the transition from total socio-economic and emotional dependence to relative independence.

3. NATURE AND SEQUENCE OF CHANGES DURING ADOLESCENCE : Adolescence is characterized by a rapid rate of growth and development. During this period the body develops in size, strength and reproductive capabilities, and the mind becomes capable of more abstract thinking. Social relationships move from being centred on the family base to a wider horizon in which peers and other adults come to play significant roles in the adolescent's life. It is also a time when new skills and knowledge are acquired and new attitudes are formed. Although the decade of life from 10 to 19 years provides a time-bound definition of adolescence, it is important to realize that the changes occurring during this period may not correspond neatly with precise ages. This is because of variations in the onset and duration of changes between individuals. Moreover, this period of transition is perceived differently by different cultures; its perception is clearly mediated by social, economic and cultural factors. Hence, the experience of adolescence differs among individuals and by sex in any given society, and by varying conditions and circumstances such as disability, illness, socioeconomic status, and poverty. 136 Peak rates of growth and development during adolescence are exceeded only by those during fetal life and infancy.

However as indicated above, in comparison with infancy and early childhood, there is much greater individual variation both in the timing of developmental milestones and in the degree of changes in rates of growth.137 Adolescence is sometimes divided into early, middle, and late periods, which are respectively the 10-14, 15-17, and 18-19-year age groups. These periods roughly correspond with the phases in physical, social, and psychological development in the transition from childhood to adulthood. While these stages are not universally accepted and vary as above, they provide a basic framework to understand adolescent development.138

4. WHAT HEALTH SERVICES DO ADOLESCENTS NEED? Adolescents have in many surveys expressed their views about what they want from health services. They want a welcoming facility, where they can "drop-in" and be attended to quickly. They insist on privacy and confidentiality and do not want to have to seek parental permission to attend. They want a service in a convenient place at a convenient time that is free or at least affordable. They want staff to treat them with respect, not judge them. They want a range of services, and not to be asked to come back or referred elsewhere. Of course, those who plan and provide services cannot only think about the wishes of adolescents – services must be appropriate and effective, and they must be affordable and acceptable for the community.

However, services for this age group must demonstrate relevance to the needs and wishes of young people. Health services play a critical role in the development of adolescents when they:

• Treat conditions that give rise to ill health or cause adolescents concern;

• Prevent and respond to health problems that can end young lives or result in chronic ill health or disability;

• Support young people who are looking for a route to good health, by monitoring progress and addressing concerns;

• Interact with adolescents at times of concern or crisis, when they are looking for a way out of their problems;

• Make links with other services, such as counseling services, which can support adolescents. Essential services Is it possible to define essential health services for adolescents? A regional consultation carried out by the Pan American Health Organization suggested that a core package for improving adolescent health and development should:

• Monitor growth and development.

• Identify and assess problems and problem behaviour, managing these where possible or, referring young people if they cannot.

• Offer information and counselling on developmental changes, personal care and ways of seeking help.

• Provide immunization. (Immunization programmes are run for young children but not for an older sister or brother. Adolescent girls need protection from rubella before they become pregnant. Vaccines are also available for meningitis, hepatitis and tetanus.)

5. WHAT MAKES HEALTH SERVICES "ADOLESCENT-FRIENDLY"? Adolescent-friendly health services represent an approach which brings together the qualities that young people demand, with the high standards that have to be achieved in the best public services. Such services are accessible, acceptable and appropriate for adolescents. They are in the right place at the right time at the right price (free where necessary) and delivered in the right style to be acceptable to young people. They are equitable because they are inclusive and do not discriminate against any sector of this young clientele on grounds of gender, ethnicity, religion, disability, social status or any other reason. Indeed, they reach out to those who are most vulnerable and those who lack services. The services are comprehensive in that they deliver an essential package of services to the whole target group.

• They are effective because they are delivered by trained and motivated healthcare providers who are technically competent, and who know how to communicate with young people without being patronizing or judgemental.

• These providers are backed up by adolescent-friendly support staff and have access to equipment, supplies and basic services.

• They also maintain a system of quality improvement so that staff are supported and remotivated to keep up their high standards.

• Finally, the services are efficient so that they do not waste money, and they record enough information to be able to monitor and improve performance.

The gold standard for adolescent-friendly health services is that they are effective, safe and affordable, they meet the individual needs of young people who return when they need to and recommend these services to friends. Even if this ideal cannot be achieved immediately, improvements bring results. Making services adolescent-friendly is not primarily about setting up separate dedicated services, although the style of some facilities may change. The greatest benefit comes from improving generic health services in local communities and by improving the competencies of health-care providers to deal effectively with adolescents.

The characteristics of adolescent-friendly health services were discussed during the global consultation process initiated by WHO in 2000 and continued during the discussions by the expert group convened by WHO in Geneva in 2001. These characteristics are intended for application sensitively in each country, bearing in mind the cultural, social, economic and political context and the need to support health-care providers to deliver the best possible service to adolescents

EIGHT

ADOLESCENTS - GROWTH AND DEVELOPMENT

Adolescence is the period of transition between childhood and adulthood. It includes some big changes—to the body, and to the way a young person relates to the world. The many physical, sexual, cognitive, social, and emotional changes that happen during this time can bring anticipation and anxiety for both children and their families. Understanding what to expect at different stages can promote healthy development throughout adolescence and into early adulthood.

Early Adolescence (Ages 10 to 13)

· During this stage, children often start to grow more quickly. They also begin to notice other body changes, including hair growth under the arms and near the genitals, breast development in females, and enlargement of the testicles in males. They usually start a year or two earlier in girls than boys, and it can be normal for some changes to start as early as age 8 for females and age 9 for males. Many girls may start their period at around age 12, on average 2-3 years after the onset of breast development.139

· These body changes can inspire curiosity and anxiety in some—especially if they do not know what to expect or what is normal. Some children may also question their gender identity at this time, and the onset of puberty can be a difficult time for transgender children.

· Early adolescents have concrete, black-and-white thinking. Things are either right or wrong, great or terrible, without much room in between. It is normal at this stage for young people to center their thinking on themselves (called "egocentrism"). As part of this, preteens and early teens are often self-conscious about their appearance and feel as though they are always being judged by their peers.

· Pre-teens feel an increased need for privacy. They may start to explore ways of being independent of their family. In this process, they may push boundaries and may react strongly if parents or guardians reinforce limits.

Middle Adolescence (Ages 14 to 17)

· Physical changes from puberty continue during middle adolescence. Most males will have started their growth spurt, and puberty-related changes continue. They may have some voice cracking, for example, as their voices lower. Some develop acne. Physical changes may be nearly complete for females, and most girls now have regular periods.139

· At this age, many teens become interested in romantic and sexual relationships. They may question and explore their sexual identity—which may be stressful if they do not have support from peers, family, or community. Another typical way of exploring sex and sexuality for teens of all genders is self-stimulation, also called masturbation.

· Many middle adolescents have more arguments with their parents as they struggle for more independence. They may spend less time with family and more time with friends. They are very concerned about their appearance, and peer pressure may peak at this age.

· The brain continues to change and mature in this stage, but there are still many differences in how a normal middle adolescent thinks compared to an adult. Much of this is because the frontal lobes are the last areas of the brain to mature—development is not complete until a person is well into their 20s! The frontal lobes play a big role in coordinating complex decision-making, impulse control, and being able to consider multiple options and consequences.

Middle adolescents are more able to think abstractly and consider "the big picture," but they still may lack the ability to apply it at the moment. For example, in certain situations, kids in middle adolescence may find themselves thinking things like: o "I'm doing well enough in math and I want to see this movie... one night of skipping studying won't matter." o "Marijuana is legal now, so it can't be that bad." While they may be able to walk through the logic of avoiding risks outside of these situations, strong emotions often continue to drive their decisions when impulses come into play.

Late Adolescents (18-21... and beyond!) Late adolescents generally have completed physical development and grown to their full adult height. They usually have more impulse control by now and may be better able to gauge risks and rewards accurately. In comparison to middle adolescents, youth in late adolescence might find themselves thinking:

*"While I do love Paul Rudd movies, I need to study for my final."

*"Even though marijuana is legal, I'm worried about how it might affect my mood and work/school performance."

Teens entering early adulthood have a stronger sense of their individuality now and can identify their values. They may become more focused on the future and base decisions on their hopes and ideals. Friendships and romantic relationships become more stable. They become more emotionally and physically separated from their family. However, many re-establish an "adult" relationship with their parents, considering them more an equal from whom to ask advice and discuss mature topics with, rather than an authority figure. 139

Intellectual and Behavioural Development

In early adolescence, children begin to develop the capacity for abstract, logical thought. This increased sophistication leads to an enhanced awareness of self and the ability to reflect on one's being. Because of the many noticeable physical changes of adolescence, this self-awareness often turns into self-consciousness, with an accompanying feeling of awkwardness.

The adolescent also has a preoccupation with physical appearance and attractiveness and a heightened sensitivity to differences from peers.140 Adolescents also apply their new reflective capabilities to moral issues. Preadolescents understand right and wrong as fixed and absolute. Older adolescents often question standards of behavior and may reject traditions—to the consternation of parents. Ideally, this reflection culminates in the development and internalization of the adolescent's moral code.

As adolescents encounter schoolwork that is more complex, they begin to identify areas of interest as well as relative strengths and weaknesses. Adolescence is a period during which young people begin to consider career options, although most do not have a clearly defined goal. Parents and clinicians must be aware of the adolescent's capabilities, help the adolescent formulate realistic expectations, and be prepared to identify impediments to learning that need remediation, such as learning disabilities, attention problems, behavior problems, or inappropriate learning environments. Parents and clinicians should facilitate apprenticeships and experiences that expose older adolescents to potential career opportunities either during school or during school vacations.

These opportunities may help adolescents focus on their career choices and future studies. Many adolescents begin to engage in risky behaviors, such as fast driving. Many adolescents begin to experiment sexually, and some may engage in risky sexual practices. Some adolescents may engage in illegal activities, such as theft and alcohol and drug use. Experts speculate that these behaviors occur in part because adolescents tend to overestimate their abilities in preparation for leaving their homes. Recent studies of the nervous system also have shown that the parts of the brain that suppress impulses are not fully mature until early adulthood.

Emotional Development

During adolescence, the regions of the brain that control emotions develop and mature. This phase is characterized by seemingly spontaneous outbursts that can be challenging for parents and teachers who often receive the brunt. Adolescents gradually learn to suppress inappropriate thoughts and actions and replace them with goal-oriented behaviors.140

The emotional aspect of growth is most trying, often taxing the patience of parents, teachers, and clinicians. Emotional lability is a direct result of neurologic development during this period, as the parts of the brain that control emotions maturely. Frustration may also arise from growth in multiple domains. A major area of conflict arises from the adolescent's desire for more freedom, which clashes with the parents' strong instincts to protect their children from harm. Parents may need help in renegotiating their roles and slowly allowing their adolescents more privileges as well as expecting them to accept greater responsibility for themselves and within the family. Communication within even stable families can be difficult and is worsened when families are divided or parents have emotional problems of their own. Clinicians can be of great help by offering adolescents and parents sensible, practical, concrete, supportive help while facilitating communication within the family.

Social and Psychologic Development

The family is the center of social life for children. During adolescence, the peer group begins to replace the family as the child's primary social focus. Peer groups are often established because of distinctions in dress, appearance, attitudes, hobbies, interests, and other characteristics that may seem profound or trivial to outsiders. Initially, peer groups are usually same-sex but typically become mixed later in adolescence. These groups assume importance to adolescents because they provide validation for the adolescent's tentative choices and support in stressful situations.

Adolescents who find themselves without a peer group may develop intense feelings of being different and alienated. Although these feelings usually do not have permanent effects, they may worsen the potential for dysfunctional or antisocial behavior. At the other extreme, the peer group can assume too much importance, also resulting in antisocial behavior. Gang membership is more common when the home and social environments are unable to counterbalance the dysfunctional demands of a peer group.140 Clinicians should screen all adolescents for mental health disorders, such as depression, bipolar disorder, and anxiety. Mental health disorders increase in incidence during this stage of life and may result in suicidal thinking or behavior.

Psychotic disorders, such as schizophrenia, although rare, most often come to attention during late adolescence. Eating disorders, such as anorexia nervosa and bulimia nervosa, are relatively common among girls and may be difficult to detect because adolescents go to great lengths to hide their behaviors and weight changes. Substance use typically begins during adolescence. More than 70% of adolescents in the United States try alcohol before they graduate high school. Binge drinking is common and leads to both acute and chronic health risks. Research has shown that adolescents who start drinking alcohol at a young age are more likely to develop an alcohol use disorder as an adult. For example, adolescents who start drinking at age 13 are 5 times more likely to develop an alcohol use disorder than those who start drinking at age 21.

Almost 50% of US adolescents try cigarettes, over 40% try electronic cigarettes, and more than 40% try marijuana while they are in high school. Use of other drugs is much less common, although misuse of prescription drugs, including drugs for pain and stimulants, is on the rise. Parents can have a strong positive influence on their children by setting a good example (eg, using alcohol in moderation, avoiding the use of illicit drugs), sharing their values, and setting high expectations regarding staying away from drugs. Parents also should teach children that prescription drugs should be used only as directed by a physician. All adolescents should be confidentially screened for substance use. 140 Appropriate advice should be given as part of routine health care because even very brief interventions by physicians and health care practitioners have been shown to decrease substance use by adolescents.

Sexuality

In addition to adapting to bodily changes, the adolescent must become comfortable with the role of adult and must put sexual urges, which can be very strong and sometimes frightening, into perspective. Some adolescents struggle with the issue of sexual identity and may be afraid to reveal their sexual orientation to friends or family members. Homosexual adolescents may face unique challenges as their sexuality develops. Adolescents may feel unwanted or unaccepted by family or peers if they express homosexual desires. Such pressure (especially during a time when social acceptance is critically important) can cause severe stress. Fear of abandonment by parents, sometimes real, may lead to dishonest or at least incomplete communication between adolescents and their parents.

These adolescents also can be taunted and bullied by their peers. Threats of physical violence should be taken seriously and reported to school officials. The emotional development of homosexual and heterosexual adolescents is best helped by supportive clinicians, friends, and family members.140 Few elements of the human experience combine physical, intellectual, and emotional aspects as thoroughly as sexuality.

Helping adolescents put sexuality into a healthy context through honest answers regarding reproduction and sexually transmitted diseases are extremely important. Adolescents and their parents should be encouraged to speak openly regarding their attitudes toward sex and sexuality; parents' opinions remain an important determinant of adolescent behavior

NINE

Behavioural Pattern in Adolescents

Adolescence is an imperfect transition period and it is a time of great physical, emotional, and social changes. However, the awareness of adolescents on the importance of health is low. It has been reported that adolescents form behaviours and attitudes toward health during this period, which may last for a lifetime.141 Besides, the beliefs or behaviours of adolescents on health are closely related to their lifelong quality of life. Dental caries occur frequently and periodontal disease may start during adolescence, thus active oral care is necessary.

Tooth brushing is the basic oral care method at this time, and the use of oral hygiene care supplies is also known to be important. Proper tooth brushing can prevent oral diseases, such as periodontal disease and dental caries, and foster the self-care ability for oral health through the changes in knowledge, attitude and behaviour. Therefore, adolescence is a time that requires the securement of the quality of life by understanding oral health care behaviours.141 The pivotal role of behaviour as one of the major determinants of oral health has been established by numerous researchers. Good oral health behaviour such as proper oral hygiene can easily prevent major oral diseases such as dental caries, periodontal diseases and oral cancer.

Adopting healthy lifestyles can thus effectively and efficiently lead to the prevention of oral diseases. In this light, oral diseases are increasingly being viewed as lifestyle disorders. Besides, there is increasing evidence that oral health-related behaviour such as sugar and tobacco consumption can also contribute to other Non-Communicable Diseases.142 The relationship between oral health and behaviour, although very important to our understanding of the disease process, should not be overemphasized. One of the major tasks for researchers is to explore why people behave the way they behave. There is a definite need to explore various factors that influence oral health behaviour.142

Behaviour and Oral health

One has to consider why there is a consistently strong relationship between poor socioeconomic status and poor oral health. Oral health-related behaviour might be one of the key factors contributing to this relationship. Poor parental education, occupation and income might act as crucial risk factors which lead to poor oral health. Parental factors such as social class, ethnicity, employment, family size have been identified as major contributing factors. These factors operate through poor oral health behaviour to adversely impact oral health outcomes.142 Oral health in adolescents is often overlooked in primary care. Oral health care is the most unmet health care need in children and adolescents.143 Adolescents have very specific oral health needs and concerns: high rates of caries, orthodontic and restoration care, increased risk of traumatic injury, and dental phobia. Other broader health issues affecting the mouth during teen years such as poor dietary habits, increased aesthetic awareness, potential alcohol and drug use, eating disorders, teen pregnancy, and other social and psychological issues.143 Adolescence offers health care providers an opportunity to address health issues with an emphasis on what matters to teenagers is a time when continuous oral management is required to maintain proper oral health. Essential habits for a lifetime of good oral health can be formed during this period; therefore, a systematic oral health management program should be developed and operated.144 As with any age group, adolescents have a variety of factors that influence their behaviour. These factors have psychologic and social components. Attitudes, values, beliefs, and self-concept are impacted by external forces such as peer pressure and parental authority and determine responses to many life situations including behaviour related to oral health care. For adolescents, the considerations related to peers are as important as (if not more important than) they are at any other time in life, despite what parents or health professionals may desire or seek to instill.145 Among the many formative issues in adolescents, determinants for health behaviours are being shaped. Areas specifically related to oral health include145 (1) Self-concept and its relationship to oral health and compliance with orthodontic care (2) Tobacco use (3) Special considerations including anorexia, bulimia, and troubled youths and (4) Health promotions. Adolescents' attitudes toward oral health can impact each of these areas.146 Issues related to oral health care can be considered from the standpoint of being related to positive health behaviour or to risk behaviours.142 Patterns of behaviour developed in adolescence can form the basis for future health. Incorporation of primary preventive behaviours such as tooth brushing, flossing, and wearing mouth guards can be important in preventing disease and protecting against injuries that have far-reaching effects. Preventing the initiation of harmful behaviour such as tobacco use can be important for future health.147

SELF-CONCEPT

Relationship to oral health

Two dimensions of self-concept have been investigated concerning dental health behaviour: self-esteem and locus of control. Self-esteem is a "personal, subjective evaluation of an individual's worth and is derived from the reflected appraisal of others and has a 'positive-negative' dimension.

"Locus of control" describes the degree to which an individual perceives that events that happen to them are causally related to their behaviour." When the perception of the causal relationship is strong, the individual is described as having an internal locus of control. If the individual's perception is that events are determined by outside forces over which there is little control, then the individual is described as having a high external locus of control. The term health locus of control has been used to refer to perceived control in the area of personal health and well-being.148 Concerning dental health behaviour, prior research has shown that people who value themselves more may take better care of themselves. Other factors such as quality of parenting and social class also may play a role.148 In a 1997 article, Macgregor and colleagues reported on the results of a large survey conducted on 12- to 16-year-olds in England. Questions sought information related to tooth brushing frequency, use of dental floss, dental visits, and whether the respondents recalled advice about tooth brushing from the previous dental visit. Besides, questions were included to assess self-esteem and health locus of control. Information on the types of newspapers in the home was used as an assessment of socioeconomic status.148 Despite some differences based on sex and age groups, the general findings of the study showed that there was a positive correlation between tooth brushing and flossing (for both sexes) and a positive relationship between tooth brushing and social group (brushing increased as socioeconomic class increased). Self-esteem was positively correlated with tooth brushing frequency for most age groups, whereas health locus of control was related for some age groups and not others. Data on flossing were not related to self-concept. Individuals with more positive self-concept were more likely to report frequent dental visits than those with a poorer view of self.148

The investigators reported that the findings of this study are consistent with prior research and implied that self-concept may play an important role in dental health behaviour. They further suggested that those who have lower self-esteem may be less likely to comply with health advice. As with any behaviour, the issues are multifaceted, and further research is warranted because the results of this study may not generalize to other groups148 In another study, Ostberg (2002) and colleagues further investigated adolescents' perception of 1. General oral health, 2. Their personal oral health, 3. Factors that influence their health, and 4. Factors that they can control. This study used a qualitative design that included a semi-structured interview format conducted by a dentist. In addition to questions about dental health attitudes and habits, social and lifestyle issues were addressed. The information obtained was analysed, coded, categorized, and compared.149

1. General oral health

Two categories of general oral health were defined as action (physical things are done to affect the condition of the mouth) and condition (the status of the mouth). The most commonly defined action was tooth brushing; two aspects of the condition were function and appearance.150

2. Personal oral health

The most outstanding criterion for evaluating personal oral health was the presence or absence of caries.150 Accounts of self-perceptions of oral health have hitherto been rare, although they are of great interest for strategies in health promotion. Anna-Lena Östberg, Kristina Jarkman, Ulf Lindblad &Arne Halling in the year 2nd July 2009 with the objective of this study was to increase our knowledge of adolescents' perceptions of oral health and influencing factors. Data was analysed according to the constant comparative method. Areas of focus were general oral health, personal oral health, dental care, and lifestyle issues. Oral health awareness was generally low among the informants.

Two categories of oral health were identified: action (the physical things we do to affect the condition of our mouths) and condition (the physical status of the mouth). Conditional aspects were most frequent in evaluations of personal oral health. Perceptions of influences on oral health were related to personal and professional care, social support and impact, and external factors. 'Concern for oral health' was derived as the core category in perceived influence on oral health. The study indicates that it is important to find factors that enhance adolescents' awareness of their resources and to seek mechanisms that govern internalization. There is a need to find strategies to convey such knowledge to the intermediaries: dental personnel and parents.

Social norms and socialization

The role of social norms, acting as important moderating and developmental influences upon the evaluative nature of beliefs, effects and behaviours, has been discussed by many researchers.151-154 The evolution of normative behaviour and beliefs, formed by socialization is also regarded as an enduring, life long process, influenced by parents teachers, peers and siblings, schools, societies and the media,155-156 that equips individuals to work with, adapt and belong to social groups. Socialization in the broadest terms refers to how individuals are assisted to develop as members of one or more social groups.

The process is seen as interactive, with new members of a group being selective in their acceptance of particular behaviours. In some circumstances, the interaction may result in the modification of the behaviour of older members.156 This interactive process is reflected in the definition of socialization by Zigler and Child (1969): Socialization is a broad term for the whole process by which an individual develops, through a transaction with other people, his specific patterns of socially relevant behaviour and experience. The outcomes of the socialization process are also suggested by 156 in their definition as 'a variety of outcomes, including the acquisition of rules, roles, standards, and values across the social, emotional, cognitive, and personal domains.'

Behaviourally, adolescence is associated with volatile emotions and boundary-testing behaviour as individuals explore and assert personal identity, learn to navigate peer relationships, and transition to independence. The strongest stereotypes of adolescence are portrayed in countless television shows and movies: the emergence of sexual interest and behaviour, and decision-making dilemmas. These behaviours are studied in the recent paper below.

Somerville and colleagues (2017) 157 had participants aged 12–28 play one-armed bandit games in which two choices that differed in average reward magnitude were presented. Each game began with four fixed choices (made by the computer). In some games, the fixed choices were evenly distributed between the two choices, so participants had the same amount of information about each choice. In other games, the fixed choices were unevenly distributed (one choice selected once, the other selected three times). The dependent variable was the choice participants made on their first free choice. Although overall levels of exploration did not vary with age, the strategic use of exploration differed from adolescence to adulthood, particularly in cases where one bandit had a higher reward value, and the other contained higher information value (i.e. fewer previous pay-outs displayed during fixed choices).

When there was only one free choice in the game, all participants generally exploited the high reward option. However, in games where participants would ultimately make six free choices, increasing age was related to an increased tendency to explore, reflected in a tendency to choose the lower value, higher information option. Thus, adolescent thinking becomes somewhat experimental in the scientific sense, employing hypotheses to test new ideas against outward reality. In formulating hypotheses about the world, adolescent cognition can be seen to grow along with formal, scientific, logical thinking.

Consider, for example, a problem of combinatorial thought: An adolescent is presented with five jars, each containing a colourless liquid. Combining the liquids from three particular jars will produce colour, whereas using the liquid from either of the two remaining jars will not produce a colour. The adolescent is told that a colour can be produced but is not shown which combination produces this effect. Children at the concrete-operational stage typically try to solve this problem by combining liquids two at a time, but after combining all pairs, or possibly trying to mix all five liquids, their search for the workable combination usually stops. An adolescent at the formal-operational stage, on the other hand, will explore all possible solutions, systematically testing all possible combinations of two and three liquids until the colour is produced. As another example, consider adolescent thinking in respect to certain types of verbal problems—for instance, as represented by the question "If Jane is taller than Doris and shorter than Francine, who is the shortest of the three?"

Concrete-operational children may be able to solve an analogous problem (e.g., one using sticks of various lengths, with the sticks present). Abstract verbal problems, however, are usually not solved until the capacity for formal operations has emerged. Formal-operational thought does not seem to be a stage characterizing all adolescents. Studies of older adolescents and adults in Western cultures show that not all individuals attain formal operations. In turn, in some non-Western groups, there is a failure ever to attain formal operations. Some researchers have attributed these differences to the differences between rural and urban societies and the different kinds of schooling offered by each.

There is, however, little evidence for socioeconomic or educational differences being associated with the achievement of formal-operational thought. These results suggest that decision-making in adolescence is not constrained by an inability to consider decision horizon, as the number of future decision choices available influenced exploration behaviour. Instead, age-related changes in decision-making strategy from adolescence to adulthood arise because of changes in the value assigned to immediate reward versus the future utility of information.

TEN

ADOLESCENT AND HYGIENE

Personal hygiene is generally defined as the cleanliness of the body and proper maintenance of personal appearance. This generally includes all body areas and clothing. Kids do not naturally understand the importance of personal hygiene and how to maintain it. The primary education of hygiene starts with the family members through which adolescents learn what to do and how to follow cleanliness rules on their own. Adolescents should be serious about hygienic practices and if they do not follow, they are teased in school or by friends for having a dirty body, dirty clothing, or greasy hair. Which indirectly lowers down their self-confidence and children feel neglected.

Therefore, Hygiene practices should be included in their daily routine.207 There are several basic types of hygiene for kids. First of all is the cleanliness of the body, which alleviates dirt and odour. A child should be taught to bathe or shower every day and to wash their hands frequently with antibacterial soap. Dr. Lynn Smitherman, a pediatrics professor at Wayne State University, stated that: "Handwashing is one of the most important cleanliness habits children can learn. At least, the child should learn to wash their hands before meals and after using the restroom. The second is oral hygiene, which means brushing the teeth regularly. It should be done at least twice a day, once in the morning and once at night. The third is wearing clean clothing.

Thus, children should learn to choose a clean outfit, including underwear, each day and to change out of play clothes if they become excessively soiled." Personal hygiene for children must be allotted according to their age group. Accordingly, adolescents can start to learn hygiene basics as toddlers. The hygiene promotion should be done on a wider scale which is a holistic approach that includes raising awareness on good hygiene behavior, including proper management of menstruation for adolescent girls. Adolescence is the right time to build on these basics: It is a time when children adopt changes in their body therefore through personal hygiene, they need to learn what changes are required for Personal hygiene as it plays a crucial role especially in the development of the adolescents.208

Puberty is the time during which a child moves through a series of significant and natural, healthy changes. These physical, psychological, and emotional changes signal that the child is moving from childhood to adolescence; when puberty starts child's brain causes sex hormones to start being released in the ovaries (girls) and testes (boys). Adolescence is a period of growth beginning with puberty and ending at the beginning of adulthood; it is a transitional stage between childhood and adulthood. In India, adolescents constitute about one-fifth of the population. Therefore, it can be considered as one of the huge segments of the total population. Although all teenagers have the same basic hygiene issues, however, girls need help to manage their periods. For example, you might need to talk with your daughter about how often to change her pad or tampon, and how to dispose of it which is hygienically so important.

Boys: Will need advice about shaving (how to do it and when to start), looking after their genitals, and about bodily fluids. For example, the father might talk to his son about wet dreams and how to clean up hygienically afterward. If it is difficult for a mother to talk with her daughter about puberty and periods, it is advisable to make an appointment with a family doctor for counseling. As well as teenagers do need extra time in the bathroom! While learning to shave or handling their periods, these hygienic activities might take a bit longer time but it is helpful to the child to have a bit more privacy. The intestinal parasite is most commonly observed among school-going children especially in developing countries. As a result of this morbidity, they are at risk of detrimental effects like poor cognitive performance and physical growth & practices of personal hygiene.

Puberty causes all kinds of changes in your body. Your skin and scalp may suddenly get oily very easily. Every day it seems you have new hair growing in different places. At times, you seem to sweat for no reason — and you may notice there are odours where you never had them before. What should you do about it? Read below for information on some hygiene basics — and learn how to deal with greasy hair, perspiration, and body hair. 209

Oily Hair

The hormones that create acne are the same ones that can make you feel like you're suddenly styling your hair with a comb dipped in motor oil. Each strand of hair has its own sebaceous (oil) gland, which keeps the hair shiny and waterproof. But during puberty, when the sebaceous glands produce extra oil, it can make your hair look too shiny, oily, and greasy.

Sweat and Body Odor

Perspiration, or sweat, comes from sweat glands that you've always had in your body. But thanks to puberty, these glands not only become more active than before, but they also begin to secrete different chemicals into the sweat that has a stronger smelling odor. You might notice this odor under your arms in your armpits. Your feet and genitals might also have new smells. The best way to keep clean is to bathe or shower every day using mild soap and warm water. This will help wash away any bacteria that contribute to the smells. Wearing clean clothes, socks, and underwear each day can also help you to feel clean.

Body Hair

Body hair in new places is something you can count on — again, it's hormones in action. You may want to start shaving some places where body hair grows, but whether you do is up to you.

Adolescent Hair Care

We have about 100,000 hairs on our heads. Each hair shaft has three layers, with the cuticle, or outside layer, protecting the two inner layers. Shiny hair is a sign of health because the layers of the cuticle lie flat and reflect light. When the scales of the cuticle lie flat they overlap tightly, so the inner layers are well protected from heat, sun, chlorine, and all the other hazards that can come from living in our environment. When hair is damaged, though, the scales may separate and hair can become dry. Because the scales on dry hair don't protect the inner two layers as well, hair can break and look dull. The type of hair a person has — whether it's straight or curly — can also affect how shiny it is. Sebum, which is the natural oil on the hair, covers straight hair better than curly hair, which is why straight hair can appear shinier.

Menstrual hygiene

Teaching menstrual hygiene to teenage girls involves guiding them to track their periods, use hygiene products such as a sanitary pad (reusable or disposable), or tampon, and their safe disposal after use. A teenage girl should also be given directions on the correct usage of these products.210

Shave safe

Teenage boys can develop a moustache or beard, depending on their hair growth. If the boy wishes to shave, then you can buy them shaving cream and a teen-friendly razor. Teach them how to shave their facial hair carefully without inflicting injuries. Similarly, teen girls, who want to remove their genital and underarm hair, need to be told about the importance of using sterilized equipment and to be careful while shaving their genital area. Also, teach them about the after-shave skincare routine and why they should not be sharing their paraphernalia with others.

Clean clothes and shoes

It is important to change clothes, especially undergarments and socks, every day. Clothes retain dead skin cells, sweat, and other body fluids that can harbor germs. Teens who wear clean clothes and shoes can effectively combat puberty-related issues such as body odour and smelly feet.

Adolescent Dental Hygiene

Dentists say that the most important part of tooth care happens at home. Brushing and flossing properly, along with regular dental check-up, can help prevent tooth decay and gum disease. If you're like most people, you don't exactly look forward to facing a dentist's drill. So wouldn't it be better to prevent cavities before they begin?

Oral hygiene habits

Regular, learned measures, by which people consciously try to maintain dental health or prevent dental diseases are regarded as dental health habits. These habits may be roughly divided into self-care-type habits and habits to use dental services. Oral hygiene, dietary habits, and the use of fluorides are typical self-care-type habits in dentistry, which are frequently studied about dental health and rarely as pure habits regarding their epidemiology. Oral hygiene procedures are done to remove the dental plaque, 211,212 which is the main factor in the etiology of periodontal disease and dental caries. This aim, however, is often indistinct for many, 213-215 which is regarded as an important factor causing poor toothbrushing.215,216 For proper oral hygiene, it is also necessary to use interdental cleaning aids, i.e. dental floss or toothpicks.217-220 For children, the technique of flossing can be taught as early as at the age of 8. 221 Toothbrushing is the most common oral hygiene measure. People are usually advised to brush their teeth once or twice a day 222 and a daily toothbrushing routine is often regarded as regular. The traditional conception has been that toothbrushing should be done twice a day.212 It has, however, been shown that complete removal of plaque every second day is compatible with the maintenance of gingival health.223,211 From the preventive point of view, careful cleaning of every surface of the teeth is crucial,211-213 but it is, however, the next goal after the initial adoption of toothbrushing as a regular habit.

Oral hygiene habits are learned in childhood. Toothbrushing is usually connected with waking up and/or going to bed. It has socially acceptable content and it often develops as an automatic habit. The process of adopting a single behavioral habit is affected by a person's earlier experience.215 Therefore toothbrushing as a health habit should be related to the person's network of social relations. The behavior of parents affects profoundly the child's behavior.224 In particular, the mother's behavior is considered important in the adoption of a health habit.225- 228

Toothpastes:

Types of toothpaste

Each type of toothpaste has its unique benefits. Some specialty types of toothpaste include:

Antimicrobial: Antimicrobial toothpaste may contain stannous fluoride, an antibacterial agent that also provides anti-cavity and sensitivity benefits.

Tartar control: Tartar-control toothpaste may contain sodium pyrophosphate which helps to keep tartar from forming on teeth or better yet, sodium hexametaphosphate, which helps prevent tartar and stains, above the gum line. But if you already have stubborn tartar, tartar control toothpaste won't remove it—you'll need a professional cleaning from your dental professional.

Whitening: Whitening toothpaste contains chemical or abrasive ingredients to help remove and/or prevent stains from forming on the teeth. When used regularly, whitening kinds of toothpaste can reduce the appearance of stains and make your teeth look whiter.

Fluoride helps prevent tooth decay by slowing the breakdown of enamel and increasing the rate of the remineralization process. The new enamel crystals that form is harder, larger, and more resistant to acid. Tooth enamel is hard yet porous. Plaque on the surface of your teeth can produce acids that seep into the pores (rods) of the enamel and break down its internal structure. This process, called demineralization, can create a weak spot in the tooth that may become a cavity if left untreated. Learning what fluoride does for the health of your teeth will help you become more aware of how to identify plaque and prevent it from becoming a cavity.

Giving Plaque the Brush-Off

To prevent cavities, you need to remove plaque, the transparent layer of bacteria that coats the teeth. The best way to do this is by brushing your teeth twice a day and flossing at least once a day. Brushing also stimulates the gums, which helps to keep them healthy and prevent gum disease. Brushing and flossing are the most important things that you can do to keep your teeth and gums healthy. Toothpaste contains abrasives, detergents, and foaming agents. Fluoride, the most common active ingredient in toothpaste, is what prevents cavities. So you should always be sure your toothpaste contains fluoride.

Toothbrushing Methods

Many methods for brushing the teeth have been described and promoted as being efficient and effective. These methods can be categorized primarily according to the pattern of motion when brushing:229 Roll: The roll method' or modified Stillman" technique Vibratory: The Stillman,"' Charters,230 or Bass" techniques Circular: The Fones 231 technique Vertical: The Leonard technique 232 Horizontal: The scrub technique.

Controlled studies evaluating the effectiveness of the most common brushing techniques have not demonstrated any clear superiority for any one method. The scrub technique is probably the simplest and most common method of brushing. Patients with periodontal disease are most frequently taught a sulcular brushing technique using a vibratory motion to improve access in the gingival areas. The roll technique seems to be the least effective method, perhaps because it generates only intermittent pressure against the teeth compared with the sustained force applied with the sulcular and scrub techniques.233 .

Three common methods of brushing the teeth are presented here, any of them, if properly performed, can provide excellent plaque control. The goal of brushing is to remove as much plaque from the accessible tooth surfaces as possible. The best brushing method for each patient is determined when forming an individualized and complete plaque control program. It also should be remembered that brushing with a powered toothbrush is an equally good alternative.

The Bass Method Technique

Place the head of a soft brush parallel with the occlusal plane, with the brush head covering three to four teeth, beginning at the most distal tooth in the arch. Place the bristles at the gingival margin, establishing an angle of 45 degrees to the long axis of the teeth. Exert gentle vibratory pressure, using short back-and-forth motions without dislodging the tips of the bristles. This motion forces the bristle ends into the gingival sulcus area as well as partially into the interproximal embrasures. The pressure should produce perceptible blanching of the gingiva.

Complete approximately 20 strokes in the same position. This repeated motion cleans the tooth surfaces, concentrating on the apical third of the clinical crowns, the gingival sulci, and as far onto the proximal surfaces as the bristles can reach. Lift the brush, move it to the adjacent teeth, and repeat the process for the next three or four teeth. Continue around the arch, brushing about three teeth at a time, then use the same method to brush the lingual surfaces. After completing the maxillary arch, move the brush to the mandibular arch and brush in the same manner until the entire dentition is completed. To help reach the lingual surfaces of the anterior teeth if the brush seems too large, insert the brush vertically.

Press the end of the brush into the gingival sulcus area and proximal surfaces at a 45-degree angle to the long axis of the teeth and brush with multiple short vibratory strokes. Press the bristles firmly into the pits and fissures of the occlusal surfaces and brush with about 20 short back-and-forth strokes. Use this technique and brush a few teeth at a time until all posterior teeth in all four quadrants are cleaned. The Bass technique requires patience and placement of the toothbrush in many different positions to cover the full dentition. Patients need to be instructed to brush in a controlled and systematic sequence to optimize plaque removal.

The Bass method has certain advantages over other techniques, as follows: 1. The short back-and-forth motion is easy to master because it is a simple movement familiar to most patients who brush using a scrub technique. 2. It concentrates the cleaning action on the cervical and interproximal portions of the teeth, where the microbial plaque is most likely to have accumulated. The Bass technique is efficient and can be recommended for any patient with or without periodontal involvement.

Interdental Cleaning Aids

Any toothbrush, regardless of the brushing method used, does not completely remove interdental plaque. This is true both in individuals with healthy periodontal conditions and those with periodontal destruction resulting in open embrasures.234,235 Interdental plaque removal is crucial to augment the effects of tooth brushing because, as previously noted, the majority of dental and periodontal disease originates in interproximal areas.

Other conditions found in periodontal and gingival diseases also demand an emphasis on interproximal cleaning. The gingival tissues are swollen in the presence of gingival inflammation, rendering the self-cleansing mechanisms of the mouthless effective than in a healthy periodontium. Also, tissue destruction associated with periodontal disease may leave large open spaces between teeth and long-exposed root surfaces with anatomical concavities and furcations. These are difficult areas to clean and only poorly accessible to the toothbrush.236 Interdental cleaning should occur every day for the same rationale as brushing daily

The purpose of interdental cleaning is to remove plaque, not to dislodge fibrous threads of food wedged between teeth. Although interdental cleaning does dislodge food fragments, correcting proximal tooth contacts and plunger cusps is required to stop chronic food impaction. The specific aids required for interproximal cleaning depend on various criteria such as the size of the interdental spaces, the presence of furcations, tooth alignment, and the presence of orthodontic appliances or fixed prostheses.

Dental Floss

Dental floss is the most widely recommended tool for removing plaque from proximal tooth surfaces." Floss is available as a multifilament nylon yarn that is twisted or non-twisted, bonded or nonbonded, waxed or unwaxed, and thick or thin. Monofilament flosses made of a Teflontype material are preferred by some individuals because they are slick and do not fray. Technique: The floss must contact the proximal surface from line angle to line angle to clean effectively. It must also clean the entire proximal surface, not just be slipped apical to the contact area. The following description is a primer in floss technique:

- Start with a piece of floss long enough to grasp securely; 12 to 18 inches is usually sufficient. It may be wrapped around the fingers, or the ends may be tied together in a loop.
- Stretch the floss tightly between the thumb and forefinger , or between both forefingers, and pass it gently through each contact area with a firm back-and-forth motion. Do not snap the floss past the contact area, because this may injure the interdental gingiva. The zealous snapping of floss through contact areas creates proximal grooves in the gingiva.
- Once the floss is apical to the contact area between the teeth, wrap the floss around the proximal surface of one tooth, and slip it under the marginal gingiva. Move the floss firmly along the tooth up to the contact area and gently down into the sulcus again, repeating this up and-down stroke several times (Fig. 49-16). Then move the floss across the interdental gingiva and repeat the procedure on the proximal surface of the adjacent tooth.
- Continue through the whole dentition, including the distal surface of the last tooth in each quadrant. When the working portion of the floss becomes soiled or begins to shred, move to a fresh portion of floss.

Interdental Brushes Interdental brushes are cone-shaped or cylindric brushes made of bristles mounted on a handle , single-tufted brushes, or small cylindric brushes. Interdental brushes are particularly suitable for cleaning large, irregular, or concave tooth surfaces adjacent to wide interdental spaces. Technique: Interdental brushes of any style are inserted through interproximal spaces and moved back and forth between the teeth with short strokes.

For most efficient cleaning, it is probably best to select the diameter of the brush that is slightly larger than the gingival embrasures to be cleaned. This size permits bristles to exert pressure on both proximal tooth surfaces, working their way into concavities on the roots. Single-tufted brushes are highly effective on the lingual surface of mandibular molars and premolars, where the tongue often impedes a regular toothbrush and may provide access to furcation areas and isolated areas of a deep recession.

Chemical Plaque Control

Mechanical plaque removal remains the primary method used to prevent dental diseases and maintain oral health. However, an improved understanding of the infectious nature of dental diseases has dramatically revitalized interest in chemical methods of plaque control.

The ADA Council on Scientific Affairs has adopted a program for acceptance of plaque control agents. The agents must be evaluated in placebo-controlled clinical trials of 6 months or longer that demonstrate significantly improved gingival health compared with controls. To date, the ADA has accepted two agents for the treatment of gingivitis: prescription solutions of chlorhexidine digluconate mouth rinse and non-prescription essential oil mouth rinse.

Chlorhexidine

The agent that has shown the most positive results to date is chlorhexidine, a diguanidohexane with pronounced antiseptic properties. The initial finding that two daily rinses with 10 ml of a 0.2% aqueous solution of chlorhexidine digluconate almost completely inhibited the development of dental plaque, calculus and gingivitis in the human model for experimental gingivitis 235 has been confirmed by several other clinical investigations.

Clinical studies of several months' duration have reported plaque reductions of 45% to 61% and, more importantly, gingivitis reductions of 27% to 67%. 68,'92 The 0.12% chlorhexidine digluconate preparation is an equally effective agent currently available in the U.S. for reducing plaque and gingivitis.

Oral Hygiene and The Nutrition Connection

Eating sugar, as you probably already know, is a major cause of tooth decay. But it's not just how much sugar you eat — when and how you eat it can be just as important to keeping teeth healthy. When you eat sugary foods or drink sodas frequently throughout the day, the enamel that protects your teeth is constantly exposed to acids. Hard candies, cough drops, and breath mints that contain sugar are especially harmful because they dissolve slowly in your mouth. Many experts suggest that you take a 3-hour break between eating foods containing sugar. Sugary or starchy foods eaten with a meal are less harmful to your teeth than when they've eaten alone, possibly because the production of saliva, which washes away the sugar and bacteria, is increased.

Eating sugary foods before you go to bed can be the most damaging (especially if you don't brush your teeth afterward) because you don't produce as much saliva when you sleep. For most people, it's hard to cut out sweets completely, so try to follow these more realistic guidelines:

• Eat carbohydrates (sugars and starches) with a meal.

• If you can't brush your teeth after eating, rinse your mouth with water or mouthwash, or chew sugarless gum. • Don't eat sugary foods between meals.

• If you snack, eat nonsugary foods, such as cheese, popcorn, raw veggies, or yogurt.

Visit the Dentist

The main reason for going to the dentist regularly — every 6 months — is prevention. The goal is to prevent tooth decay, gum disease, and other disorders that put the health of your teeth and mouth at risk.

Your first consultation with a dentist will probably consist of three main parts: a dental and medical history (where the dentist or dental hygienist asks you questions about your tooth care and reviews any dental records), a dental examination, and professional cleaning. The dentist will examine your teeth, gums, and other mouth tissues. He or she may also examine the joints of your jaws. The dentist will use a mirror and probe (a metal pick-like instrument) to check the crown (visible part) of each tooth for plaque and evidence of looseness or decay. The dentist also will check your bite and the way your teeth fit together (called occlusion). Your dentist will examine the general condition of your gums, which should be firm and pink, not soft, swollen, or inflamed.

He or she (or an assistant) will use the probe to check the depth of the sulcus, the slight depression where each tooth meets the gum. Deep depressions, called pockets, are evidence of gum disease. After examining the visible parts of your teeth and mouth, your dentist will take X-rays that might reveal tooth decay, abscesses (collections of pus surrounded by swollen tissue), or impacted wisdom teeth. Professional cleaning is usually performed by a dental hygienist, a specially trained and licensed dental professional. Cleaning consists mainly of removing hard deposits using a scaler (a scraping instrument) or an ultrasonic machine, which uses high-frequency sound waves to loosen plaque deposits. The particles are then rinsed off with water. After cleaning, the dental hygienist will polish your teeth.

The process cleans and smoothens the surfaces of the teeth, removing stains and making it harder for plaque to stick to the teeth. Finally, the hygienist may treat your teeth with a fluoride compound or a sealant to help prevent decay. At the end of your visit, the dentist will let you know if you need to return to fill a cavity. Your dentist also may refer you to an orthodontist if he or she thinks you may need braces or have other issues. Dental caries (tooth decay) can attack the teeth at any age.

84% of 17- year-olds have the disease. Left untreated, caries can cause severe pain and result in tooth loss. Losing teeth affects how you look and feel about yourself as well as your ability to chew and speak. Treating caries is also expensive. So prevention and early treatment are important. It may surprise you to know that 60% of 15-year-olds experience gingivitis, the first stage of gum disease.

Gingivitis, which involves the gums but not the underlying bone and ligament, is almost always caused by an accumulation of plaque. As with caries, treatment can be expensive. If you remove plaque regularly and follow good oral hygiene habits, your gums usually will return to their healthy state. However, more serious gum disease can cause gums to swell, turn red, and bleed, and sometimes causes discomfort. How dentists treat gum disease depends on the extent of the disease.

Why do Teens Face Personal Hygiene Issues?

The following are some of the common causes for teens to face personal hygiene issues.

1. Lack of awareness: This is one of the most common reasons for a teen to show disinterest in personal hygiene. The teen may not be aware of the importance of hygiene and the steps they need to take in this regard.

2. Habit of procrastination: They may tend to postpone their bath or avoid taking a bath or brushing their hair if they have no plans of going out for the day. They may take it easy on washing their hands after using the toilet or before eating. These instances might be fewer in teens who have been oriented into personal hygiene from a younger age itself.

3. Delay in cognitive development or mental health problems: Some teens may have an issue in maintaining a basic hygiene routine due to cognitive development delay or some mental health problems such as depression. In such special cases, either the teen is not able to understand the importance of personal hygiene, or they forget the steps to perform the practice. Teens with cognitive delays and mental health issues should see a medical professional establish a hygiene regimen. In other cases, it is advisable to speak to your teen and make them understand the importance of personal hygiene.

How To Talk To Your Teen About Personal Hygiene?

You may the following steps to talk to a teen about personal hygiene.

1. The best phase to strike a conversation about personal hygiene is at the beginning of puberty. It can ensure that by the time your tween enters adolescence, they are well-prepared for the changes they might experience.

2. Do a quick research on the issue that you want to discuss. It will help you share correct information with your teen.

3. Pick a quiet and alone time for the conversation. A teen who is at ease can participate in the conversation comfortably.

4. Keep the participants of the conversation limited to you and the teen to respect their privacy. It will also help your teen develop trust in you, and they will likely confide in you in the future as well.

5. Share your observations and tell them how poor hygiene habits could become a problem. However, while talking, ensure that you do not make it seem shameful and embarrassing. It is good to start your conversation by praising your teen and then slowly progress to the areas of improvement.

6. Share about the social aspects of hygiene. Share live examples and be a role model. Guide them with examples of how hygiene is important for physical, physiological, mental, and social health. For example, when you talk about oral hygiene activities, talk about a relative or friend, who ended up going for a root canal treatment because they were not brushing and flossing their teeth.

7. Once you have shared your part, ask your tween or teen if they have any questions or suggestions to make. Listen to them patiently and make them feel heard. Try to answer what you can and show that you are willing to help them.

8. Be supportive and continue to communicate about their personal needs. Bring them all necessary personal hygiene items as per their needs. Take your teen along for shopping for their personal care products.

9. Praise and reward the teen appropriately when you see positive changes. If the teen does not improve, then set some strict hygiene rules.

10. Seek a professional's help if you observe any erratic behavior related to personal hygiene that you cannot talk out.

Personal hygiene is an inevitable part of overall health. It is good to guide your teen about the importance of personal hygiene while they are in their pre-teens or tweens. Since transitioning from childhood to adolescence is not smooth for every child, ensure that you are their guiding support to the best of your capacity.

Patience and perseverance will help your child develop a routine of healthy hygiene. A commitment to action has been articulated to address the global burden of disease from inadequate water, sanitation, and hygiene.237,238 Poor personal hygiene is one of the ten leading behavioral risk factors attributing to a large share of this disease burden.239 S

tudies have shown that without good hygiene behavior adequate sanitation and water supply alone leads only to minor health improvements.240,241 Promoting optimal hygiene behavior is now recognized as an issue in its own right, with an understanding that adequate tooth brushing and hand washing are cost-effective ways of reducing and preventing diarrhea, trachoma, schistosomiasis, infectious hepatitis, dental plaque and caries, periodontal diseases, and other fecal-oral diseases.238,241-245

While poor personal hygiene practices among children and adolescents in low- and middle-income countries are largely preventable, effective public health programs would need to build on profiling those most at risk and on understanding what key social and demographic factors will contribute to sustainable changes in hygiene practices. The majority of available data on the determinants of hygiene behavior in adolescents so far have come from European countries and most have focused on dental hygiene. 246-251

These studies have shown that toothbrushing is more common in girls and older adolescents. 246,248,250 Adolescents from higher socio-economic backgrounds, with better school performance and high self-esteem, also had better toothbrushing frequency.248,250-252 One study reported that both smokers and non-smokers who frequently toothbrushes tended to perform handwashing more often after toilet use.253 The few studies from low- and middle-income countries also found that tooth brushing behavior is associated with gender, parental socioeconomic status, and education. 242,244

ELEVEN

ORAL HEALTH CARE NEEDS & MANAGEMENT OF ADOLESCENTS

The adolescent patient is recognized as having distinctive needs254,255 due to:

(1) a potentially high caries rate
(2) increased risk for traumatic injury and periodontal disease
(3) a tendency for poor nutritional habits
(4) an increased aesthetic desire and awareness
(5) complexity of combined orthodontic and restorative care (e.g., congenitally missing teeth)
(6) dental phobia
(7) the potential use of tobacco, alcohol, and other drugs
(8) pregnancy
(9) eating disorders and
(10) unique social and psychological needs.256,257

Treatment of the adolescent patient can be multi-faceted and complex. Accurate, comprehensive, and up-to-date medical and social histories are necessary for correct diagnosis and effective treatment planning. Familiarity with the patient's medical history is essential for decreasing the risk of aggravating a medical condition while rendering dental care. If the parent is unable to provide adequate details regarding a patient's medical history, consultation with the medical health care provider may be indicated. The practitioner also may need to obtain additional information confidentially from an adolescent patient.

Recommendations

This guideline addresses some of the special needs within the adolescent population and proposes general recommendations for their management.

Caries

Adolescence marks a period of significant caries activity for many individuals. Research suggests that the overall caries rate is declining, yet remains highest during adolescence.258,259 Immature permanent tooth enamel,260 a total increase in susceptible tooth surfaces, and environmental factors such as diet, independence to seek care or avoid it, a low priority for oral hygiene, and additional social factors also may contribute to the upward slope of caries during adolescence.261 The dental provider needs to emphasize the positive effects that fluoridation, professional topical fluoride treatment, routine professional care, patient education, and personal hygiene can have in counteracting the changing pattern of caries in the adolescent population.256,257

Management of Caries

Primary prevention

Fluoride: Fluoridation has proven to be the most economical and effective caries prevention measure. The adolescent can benefit from fluoride throughout the teenage years and into early adulthood. Although the systemic benefit of fluoride incorporation into developing enamel is not considered necessary past 16 years of age, topical benefits can be obtained through optimally-fluoridated water, professionally-applied and prescribed compounds, and fluoridated dentifrices.262,263 Recommendations: The adolescent should receive maximum fluoride benefit dependent on risk assessment:263

· brushing teeth twice a day with a fluoridated dentifrice is recommended to provide continuing topical benefits.264

· professionally-applied fluoride treatments should be based on the individual patient's caries-risk assessment, as determined by the patient's dental provider.263,264

· home-applied prescription-strength topical fluoride products [e.g., 0.4 percent stannous fluoride gel, 0.5 percent fluoride gel or paste, 0.2 percent sodium fluoride (NaF) rinse] may be used when indicated by an individual's caries pattern or caries risk status.264

· systemic fluoride intake via optimal fluoridation of drinking water or professionally-prescribed supplements is recommended to 16 years of age. Supplements should be given only after all other sources of fluoride have been evaluated.264

Oral hygiene:

Adolescence can be a time of heightened caries activity and periodontal disease due to an increased intake of cariogenic substances and inattention to oral hygiene procedures.265 Toothbrushing with a fluoridated dentifrice and flossing can provide benefit through the topical effect of the fluoride and plaque removal from tooth surfaces.266

.

Recommendations:

· adolescents should be educated and motivated to maintain personal oral hygiene by daily plaque removal, including flossing, with the frequency and technique based on the individual's disease pattern and oral hygiene needs.265,266

· professional removal of plaque and calculus is recommended highly for the adolescent, with the frequency of such intervention based on the individual's assessed risk for caries/periodontal disease, as determined by the patient's dental provider.266

Diet management:

Many adolescents are exposed to and consume high quantities of refined carbohydrates and acid-containing beverages.261,267 The adolescent can benefit from diet analysis and modification.

Recommendations: Diet analysis, along with professionally determined recommendations for maximal general and dental health, should be part of an adolescent's dental health management.268

Sealants:

Sealant placement is an effective caries-preventive technique that should be considered on an individual basis. Sealants have been recommended for any tooth, primary or permanent, that is judged to be at risk for pit and fissure caries.257,270 Caries risk may increase due to changes in patient habits, oral microflora, or physical condition, and unsealed teeth subsequently might benefit from sealant applications.270

Recommendations: Adolescents at risk for caries should have sealants placed. An individual's caries risk may change over time; periodic reassessment for sealant need is indicated throughout adolescence.270

Secondary prevention

Professional preventive care: Professional preventive dental care, on a routine basis, may prevent oral disease or disclose existing disease in its early stages. The adolescent patient whose oral health has not been monitored routinely by a dentist may have advanced caries, periodontal disease, or other oral involvement urgently in need of professional evaluation and extensive treatment.

Recommendations:

· timing of periodic oral examinations should take into consideration the individual's needs and risk indicators to determine the most cost-effective, disease-preventive benefit to the adolescent.

• an initial and periodic radiographic examination should be a part of a clinical evaluation. The type, number, and frequency of radiographs should be determined only after an oral examination and history taking. Previously exposed radiographs should be available, whenever possible, for comparison. Currently accepted guidelines for radiographic exposures (i.e., appropriate films based upon medical history, caries risk, history of periodontal disease, and growth and development assessments) should be followed.271

Restorative dentistry: In cases where remineralization of non-cavitated, demineralized tooth surfaces is not successful, as demonstrated by the progression of carious lesions, dental restorations are necessary. Preservation of tooth structure, aesthetics, and each patient's needs must be considered when selecting a restorative material.272 Molars with extensive caries or malformed, hypoplastic enamel—for which traditional amalgam or composite resin restorations are not feasible— may require full coverage restorations.270 Small non-cavitated interproximal carious lesions and facial post orthodontic white spot lesions may be treated by resin infiltration.270

Recommendations: Each adolescent patient and restoration must be evaluated on an individual basis. Preservation of non-carious tooth structure is desirable. Referral should be made when treatment needs are beyond the treating dentist's scope of practice.270

Periodontal diseases

Adolescence can be a critical period in the human being's periodontal status. Epidemiologic and immunologic data suggest that irreversible tissue damage from periodontal disease begins in late adolescence and early adulthood.273 Adolescents have a higher prevalence of gingivitis than prepubertal children or adults. The rise of sex hormones during adolescence is suspected to be a cause of the increased prevalence. Studies suggest that the increase in sex hormones during puberty affects the composition of the subgingival microflora.36 Other studies suggest circulating sex hormones may alter capillary permeability and increase fluid accumulation in the gingival tissues. This inflammatory gingivitis is believed to be transient as the body accommodates the ongoing presence of sex hormones.275

Conditions affecting the adolescent include, but are not limited to, gingivitis, puberty gingivitis, hyperplastic gingivitis related to orthodontic therapy, gingival recession that may or may not be related to orthodontic therapy, drug-related gingivitis, pregnancy gingivitis, necrotizing ulcerative gingivitis, localized aggressive periodontitis, and periodontitis.274,275 Personal oral hygiene and regular professional intervention can minimize the occurrence of these conditions and prevent irreversible damage.

Recommendations: The adolescent will benefit from an individualized preventive dental health program, which includes the following items aimed specifically at periodontal health:

• patient education emphasizing the etiology, characteristics, and prevention of periodontal diseases, as well as self-hygiene skills.275

• a personal, age-appropriate oral hygiene program including plaque removal, oral health self-assessment, and diet. Sulcular brushing and flossing should be included in plaque removal, and frequent follow-up to determine the adequacy of plaque removal and improvement of gingival health should be considered.275

• regular professional intervention, the frequency of which should be based on individual needs and should include evaluation of personal oral hygiene success, periodontal status, and potential complicating factors such as medical conditions, malocclusion, or handicapping conditions. Periodontal probing, periodontal charting, and radiographic periodontal diagnosis should be a consideration when caring for the adolescent. The extent and nature of the periodontal evaluation should be determined professionally on an individual basis. Those patients with progressive periodontal disease should be referred when the treatment needs are beyond the treating dentist's scope of practice.275

• appropriate evaluation for procedures to facilitate orthodontic treatment including, but not limited to, tooth exposure, frenectomy, fiberotomy, gingival augmentation, and implant placement.276

Occlusal considerations

Malocclusion can be a significant treatment need in the adolescent population as both environmental and/or genetic factors come into play. Although the genetic basis of many malocclusions makes it unpreventable, numerous methods exist to treat the occlusal disharmonies, temporomandibular joint dysfunction, periodontal disease, and disfiguration which may be associated with malocclusion. Within the area of occlusal problems are several tooth/ jaw-related discrepancies that can affect the adolescent. Third molar malposition and temporomandibular disorders require special attention to avoid long-term problems. Congenitally missing teeth present complex problems for the adolescent and often require combined orthodontic and restorative care for a satisfactory resolution.

Malocclusion:

Any tooth/jaw positional problems that present significant aesthetic, functional, physiologic, or emotional dysfunction are potential difficulties for the adolescent. These can include single or multiple tooth malpositions, tooth/jaw size discrepancies, and craniofacial disfigurements. Recommendations: Malposition of teeth, malrelationship of teeth to jaws, tooth/jaw size discrepancy, skeletal malrelationship, or craniofacial malformations or disfigurement that presents functional, aesthetic, physiologic, or emotional problems for the adolescent should be referred for evaluation when the treatment needs are beyond the treating dentist's scope of practice. Treatment of malocclusion by a dentist should be based on professional diagnosis, available treatment options, patient motivation and readiness, and other factors to maximize progress.277

Third molars: Third molars can present acute and chronic problems for the adolescent. Impaction or malposition leading to such problems as pericoronitis, caries, cysts, or periodontal problems merits evaluation for removal.278 The role of the third molar as a functional tooth also should be considered.

Recommendations: Evaluation of third molars, including radiographic diagnostic aids, should be an integral part of the dental examination of the adolescent.271 For diagnostic and extraction criteria, refer to AAPD's Guideline on Paediatric Oral Surgery.278 Referral should be made if treatment is beyond the treating dentist's scope of practice.

Temporomandibular joint (TMJ) problems:

Disorders of the TMJ can occur at any age, but symptoms appear more prevalent in adolescence.279

Recommendations: Evaluation of the TMJ and related structures should be a part of the examination of the adolescent. An adolescent comprehensive dental examination should include a screening evaluation of the TMJ and surrounding area. This evaluation will include a screening history for symptoms, clinical examination, and evaluation of jaw movements, and if indicated, radiographic imaging. Referral should be made when the diagnostic and/or treatment needs are beyond the treating dentist's scope of practice.278,279

Congenitally missing teeth:

The impact of a congenitally missing permanent tooth on the developing dentition can be significant.254,280 When treating adolescent patients with congenitally missing teeth, many factors must be taken into consideration including, but not limited to, aesthetics, patient age, and growth potential, as well as orthodontic, periodontal, and oral surgical needs. 277,280

Recommendations: Evaluation of congenitally missing permanent teeth should include both immediate and long-term management. Referral should be made when the treatment needs are beyond the treating dentist's scope of practice. Due to the complexity of the growing adolescent, a team approach may be indicated.280,281

Ectopic eruption: Abnormal eruption patterns of the adolescent's permanent teeth can contribute to root resorption, bone loss, gingival defects, space loss, and aesthetic concerns. Early diagnosis and treatment of ectopically erupting teeth can result in a healthier and more aesthetic dentition. Prevention and treatment may include extraction of deciduous teeth, surgical intervention, and/or endodontic, orthodontic, periodontal, and/or restorative care.282

Recommendations: The dentist should be proactive in diagnosing and treating ectopic eruption and impacted teeth in the young adolescent. Early diagnosis, including appropriate radiographic examination,271 is important. Referral should be made when the treatment needs are beyond the treating dentist's scope of practice.281

Traumatic injuries

The most common injuries to permanent teeth occur secondary to falls, followed by traffic accidents, violence, and sports.283 All sporting activities have an associated risk of orofacial injuries due to falls, collisions, and contact with hard surfaces.284 The administrators of youth, high school, and college organized sports have demonstrated that dental and facial injuries can be reduced significantly by introducing mandatory protective equipment such as face guards and mouthguards. Additionally, youths participating in leisure activities such as skateboarding, roller skating, and bicycling also benefit from appropriate protective equipment.285

Recommendations: Dentists should introduce a comprehensive trauma prevention program to help reduce the incidence of traumatic injury to adolescent dentition. This prevention plan should consider an assessment of the patient's sport or activity, including level and frequency of activity.286 Once this information is acquired, recommendation and fabrication of an age-appropriate, sport-specific, and properly-fitted mouthguard/faceguard can be initiated.286 Players should be warned about altering the protective equipment that will disrupt the fit of the appliance. Also, players and parents must be informed that injury may occur, even with properly fitted protective equipment.286

Additional considerations in oral/dental management of the adolescent

The adolescent can present particular psychosocial characteristics that impact the health status of the oral cavity, care-seeking, and compliance. The self-concept development process, emergence of independence, and the influence of peers are just a few of the psychodynamic factors impacting dental health during this period.256.262

Aesthetic concerns: The desire to improve aesthetics of the dentition by tooth whitening and removal of stained areas or defects can be a concern of the adolescent. Indications for the appropriate use of tooth-whitening methods and products are dependent upon correct diagnosis and consideration of eruption pattern of the permanent dentition.287 The dentist must determine the appropriate mode of treatment. Use of bleaching agents, microabrasion, placement of aesthetic restoration, or a combination of treatments all can be considered.288,289

Recommendations: For the adolescent patient, judicious use of bleaching can be considered part of a comprehensive, sequenced treatment plan that takes into consideration the patient's dental developmental stage, oral hygiene, and caries status. A dentist should monitor the bleaching process, ensuring the least invasive, most effective treatment method. Dental professionals also should consider possible side effects when contemplating dental bleaching for adolescent patients.289

Tobacco use:

Significant oral, dental, and systemic health consequences and death are associated with all current forms of tobacco use. These include the use of products such as cigars, cigarettes, snus, hookahs, smokeless tobacco, pipes, bidis, kreteks, dissolvable tobacco, and electronic cigarettes.290 Smoking and smokeless tobacco use are initiated and established primarily during adolescence.291

Recommendations: The oral and systemic consequences of all current forms of tobacco use should be part of each patient's oral health education. For those adolescent patients who use tobacco products, the practitioner should provide or refer the patient to appropriate educational and counseling services.292 Supplemental medical history questions regarding tobacco use should be added to the adolescent dental record.293When associated pathology is present, referral should be made when the treatment needs are beyond the treating dentist's scope of practice.

Psychosocial and other considerations:

Behavioural considerations when treating an adolescent may include anxiety, phobia, and intellectual dysfunction.1 Referral should be made when the treatment needs are beyond the treating dentist's scope of practice and consultation with nondental professionals or a team approach may be indicated. Additional examples of oral problems associated with adolescent behaviors include, but are not limited to:

- oral manifestations of sexually transmitted diseases.
- effects of oral contraceptives or antibiotics on periodontal structures.
- perimyolysis (severe enamel erosion) in bulimia.294
- traumatic injury to teeth and oral structures in athletic or other activities (short and long-term management).285,295
- intraoral and perioral piercing with possible local and systemic effects.296

The impact of psychosocial factors relating to oral health must include consideration of the following:

- changes in dietary habits (e.g., fads, freedom to snack, increased energy needs, access to carbohydrates).
- use of tobacco, alcohol, and drugs.
- motivation for maintenance of good oral hygiene.
- potential for traumatic injury

· adolescent as responsible for care.

· lack of knowledge about periodontal disease.

Physiologic changes also can contribute to significant oral concerns in adolescent. These changes include

(1) loss of remaining primary teeth;

(2) eruption of remaining permanent teeth;

(3) gingival maturity;

(4) facial growth; and

(5) hormonal changes.

Recommendations:

· an adolescent's oral health care should be provided by a dentist who has appropriate training in managing the patient's specific needs. Referral should be made when the treatment needs are beyond the treating dentist's scope of practice. This may include both dental and non-dental problems.297

· supplemental medical history topics regarding questions on pregnancy, alcohol and drug use, oral piercings, tobacco use, sexual activity, and eating disorders should be included in the adolescent dental record.

· attention should be given to the particular psychosocial aspects of adolescent dental care. Other issues such as assent, confidentiality, and compliance should be addressed in the care of these patients.293

· A complete oral health care program for the adolescent requires an educational component that addresses the particular concerns and needs of the adolescent patient and focuses on:

· — specific behaviourally-and physiologically-induced oral manifestations in this age group;266

· — shared responsibility for care and health by the adolescent, paper, and provider;266 and

· — consequences of adolescent behavior on oral health.298 Transitioning to adult care: As adolescent patients approach the age of a majority, it is important to educate the patient and parent on the value of transitioning to a dentist who is knowledgeable in adult oral health care.

The adult's oral health needs may go beyond the scope of the paediatric dentist's training. The transitioning adolescent should continue professional oral health care in an environment sensitive to his/ her individual needs. Many adolescent patients independently will choose the time to seek care from a general dentist and may elect to seek treatment from a parent's primary care provider.

In some instances, however, the treating paediatric dentist will be required to suggest transfer to adult care. Paediatric dentists are concerned about decreased access to oral health care for persons with special health care needs (SHCN)299 as they transition beyond the age of majority. Paediatric hospitals, by imposing age restrictions, can create a barrier to care for these patients. Transitioning to a dentist who is knowledgeable and comfortable with adult oral health care needs often is difficult due to a lack of trained providers willing to accept the responsibility of caring for SHCN patients.

Recommendations: At a time agreed upon by the patient, parent, and paediatric dentist, the patient should be transitioned to a dentist knowledgeable and comfortable with managing that patient's specific oral care needs. For the SHCN patient, in cases where it is not possible or desired to transition to another practitioner, the dental home can remain with the paediatric dentist and appropriate referrals for specialized dental care should be recommended when needed.299

TWELVE

TRENDS IN ORAL HEALTH

The dental profession has for many years used clinical indices to measure oral health and determine the outcome, familiar examples are the number of decayed, missing, and filled teeth, periodontal pocket depth on probing, and the presence of plaque or calculus (e.g. the CPITN or the BPI). Whilst these indicate the pathophysiology of dental disease, they fail to take account of the patient's perspective and impact of oral problems on their day-to-day life.

They are clear measures of disease rather than health. Clinical indicators remain an essential component of oral assessment, particularly in children and young adults for whom elimination of the disease is often both possible and beneficial. However, alone they cannot capture the overall impact of oral disease as they essentially only reflect the end-point of the disease process, leaving the patient's perspective of their oral health largely unknown. A more complete assessment can only be determined by incorporating the patient's self-reported perception of their oral health. This aspect is especially relevant amongst an older population who are increasingly dentate, but for whom a clinically perfect mouth is often neither possible nor desirable.

It would be particularly helpful in this new environment to acknowledge that a broader concept of oral health is necessary, one which includes the patient's ratings and perceptions of their health. This involves recording the impact of dental disease and the interventions used to treat dental disease on people's daily lives, in other words, their health-related quality of life (HR-QoL). In the 1970s, it became clear that there was a need for these QoL measures, to define the social and psychological consequences of oral disorders.300 Research in this area revealed that patients appeared to base their oral health perceptions on functional concerns,301 which demonstrated only a weak relationship with clinical assessment. In other words, patients and dentists have often used different criteria to assess oral health.

Rosenberg and Kaplan found that whilst the periodontal status and the number of dental symptoms explained some of the self-reported dental health statuses, the DMFT values did not.302 Cushing et al. also reported inconsistent associations between clinical indices and the social impact of dental disease.303 These alternative HR-QoL measures, based on patient's perceptions have come some way since this early work and are of increasing relevance to dentists:

·

· The measures could be useful to dentists for monitoring and auditing their work.

· They may be used by administrators who run health services (or insurance companies) as ways of measuring the effectiveness of dentists and dental services and as a way of prioritizing different dental needs when allocating resources.

· They may be useful as outcome measures in clinical trials of new techniques and materials. The compartmentalization involved in viewing the mouth separately from the rest of the body must cease because oral health affects general health by causing considerable pain and suffering and by changing what people eat, their speech, and their quality of life and well-being.

Oral health also affects other chronic diseases.304 Because of the failure to tackle social and material determinants and incorporate oral health into general health promotion, millions suffer intractable toothache and poor quality of life and end up with few teeth. Health policies should be reoriented to incorporate oral health using socio-dental approaches to assessing needs and the common risk factor approach for health promotion.304,305

Oral diseases are the most common chronic diseases and are important public health problems because of their prevalence, their impact on individuals and society, and the expense of their treatment. The determinants of oral diseases are known — they are the risk factors common to several chronic diseases: diet and dirt (hygiene), smoking, alcohol, risky behaviors causing injuries, and stress — and effective public health methods are available to prevent oral diseases. In some countries, oral diseases are the fourth most expensive diseases to treat.

Treating caries, estimated at 2,58,714 INR per 1000 children, would exceed the total health budget for children of most low-income countries. 306 The situation for adults in developing countries is worse, as they suffer from the accumulation of untreated oral diseases. There are few efficient dental care systems to cope with their problems, and where there are, the cost is beyond most people's means. Millions with untreated caries have cavities and suppuration, yet planners continue to overlook oral diseases, despite their significant impact on cost and quality of life. This oversight will lead to more decay and expensive, ineffective clinical interventions.

Oral health affects people physically and psychologically and influences how they grow, enjoy life, look, speak, chew, taste food, and socialize, as well astheir feelings of social well-being.305 Severe caries detracts from children's quality of life: they experience pain, discomfort, disfigurement, acute and chronic infections, and eating and sleep disruption as well as a higher risk of hospitalization, high treatment costs, and loss of school days with the consequently diminished ability to learn. Caries affects nutrition, growth, and weight gain.

Children of three years of age with nursing caries weighed about 1 kg less than control children308 because toothache and infection alter eating and sleeping habits, dietary intake, and metabolic processes. Disturbed sleep affects gluco-steroid production. Besides, there is a suppression of hemoglobin from depressed erythrocyte production. Ninety percent of pre-adolescents reported an impact related to oral health.309 Prevalence of dental pain was found to be about 33% among Brazilian teenagers, of whom 9% reported distressing, excruciating pain.310 Toothache leads to school absence, which is a ready indicator of children's health. In the USA, where caries is lower than elsewhere, visits or dental problems accounted for 117 000 hours of school lost per 100 000 children.311

Because most school dental services work mainly during school hours, the loss of schooling among the poor, who have higher caries rates, is high. In Thailand, 74% of 35–44-year olds had daily performances affected by their oral state: 46% reported their emotional stability was affected.312 Dental problems that cause chewing to be painful affect intake of dietary fiber and some nutrient-rich foods; consequently, serum levels of beta carotene, folate, and vitamin C were significantly lower in those with poorer oral status.313

Contemporary concepts of health suggest that oral health should be defined in general physical, psychological, and social well-being terms to oral status. Cohen & Jago consider the greatest contribution of dentistry is to improve quality of life.300 Disruptions in physical, psychological, and social functioning are therefore important in assessing oral health. Traditional measures use mainly clinical indices, though there are alternatives using measures of oral health-related quality of life in socio-dental approaches to assessing need.314 Chronic diseases such as obesity, diabetes, and caries are increasing in developing countries, with the implication that quality of life-related to oral health, as well as the general quality of life, may deteriorate.

Because oral and other chronic diseases have determinants in common, more emphasis should be on the common risk factor approach. The key concept underlying future oral health strategies isintegration with this approach, a major benefit being the focus on improving health conditions in general for the whole population and groups at high risk, thereby reducing social inequities. By integrating oral health into strategies for promoting general health and by assessing oral needs in socio-dental ways, health planners can greatly enhance both general and oral health. Certain recent epidemiological studies indicate a reduction in the occurrence of caries in Latin America, which is in line with the trend observed in industrialized countries in the last decades.

Despite this reduction, a polarized distribution of the disease has been observed. In adolescents and adults, the reduction observed has been less pronounced, with the great concern being maintained for the occurrence of caries in other age groups above the age of 12. Due to changes in the pattern of distribution of this disease, other aggravating circumstances in oral health have gained prominence, among them the concern being periodontal disease whose prevalence has increased.

In addition to the prevalence of oral diseases, the physical and psychological influence of these aggravating circumstances in the lives of individuals must be considered, concerning their joy of living, the possibility of speaking, the capability of chewing, and social insertion. Epidemiological studies in dentistry should monitor the population trends for the several aggravating circumstances to oral health and its interference in the quality of life.

These studies should further aid in the planning of oral health programs to address the health needs observed. Clinical indicators are important for the assessment of oral health and treatment needs, nevertheless, their limitations must be considered.311 The associated clinical and subjective indicators define a multi-dimensional assessment of the oral health condition. The quality-of-life indicators related to oral health was defined as the measurements of how dental problems and oral disorders interfere in the normal functioning of an individual's life.

Although dental caries is one of the most commonly studied oral diseases, most population studies in Brazil are concentrated in school-age children, and there is insufficient data about the prevalence of dental caries and other oral diseases in adolescents and its impact on the quality of life.

Classically, adolescence is associated with four basic needs:

(1) to find an identity;

(2) to accept sexuality and find the sexual role;

(3) to establish independence from the family; and

(4) to establish a career or vocational choice.

These needs translate into several characteristics that are often associated with this period of life. Only the naive would assume that all adolescents fit this mold or that these characteristics apply to all ages included under the definition of adolescence. Look at these characteristics as possible bases of adolescent behavior rather than as descriptions apply to all teenagers.315

First, peers are important. Many, but not all, adolescents look to peers for advice, support, recognition, and acceptance. This facet of adolescent psychology has both good and bad points. If a teenager values peer opinion, emulation of peer behavior and acceptance of peer recommendations may follow. Smoking often grows out of peer influence. Outstanding academic and athletic performance are also peer-regulated to some degree. However, not all adolescents look to peers for guidance; many still seek answers from the source that has served them well before, the family.

Second, fads may be a common part of life. Adolescence is a time for trying new things, including drugs, sex, alcohol, and tobacco on the one hand, and classical music, drama, love, and personal responsibility for health care on the other. When well directed, faddism is a learning method and can shape positive behaviors-like good oral hygiene that become the habits of adulthood. If fads are seen as ways of sampling the environment, they become less threatening, especially to parents.

Third, values may be of short duration, but their durational expectancy is as long as for other age groups. Said more simply, teenagers believe that their perception of things is "the way it is," yet that perception may change within a short time. However, if questioned about their values, many adolescents will state that their beliefs will probably remain the same for a long time.

Fourth, adolescents are viewed as a separate culture by many elements of society. From literature, one gets a distinct impression that a generation gap exists. Teenagers are the fodder for much of the output of the television and film industry. Advertisers see the teenage market as distinct and as one of the most lucrative because of the access to spending money that adolescents enjoy today. Viewing all teenagers as representatives of a subculture creates a functional gap that can escalate to confrontation, a reality illustrated by the anti-war conflicts of the sixties. On a one-to-one basis, the presumption of an adolescent's goals or motives by an adult prevents the communication that is recognized as important for successful health care.

The member countries of the WHO have decided to adopt a global strategy for achieving health for all in the year 2000. As a part of this goal, the FDI has decided to participate with 'goals for oral health in the year 2000'. The FDI already has many joint activities with WHO, serving as a link between that organization and the national dental member associations.

One joint activity is the International Collaborative Study of Dental Manpower Systems. Another is the joint working group set up to look into The Changing Patterns in Oral Health. An important task associated with this study is the project on the International Deployment of Dental Manpower investigating the uneven distribution of dental manpower between various parts of the world, especially between industrialized and developing countries.

For all these projects it is necessary to have the support of the Federation's national member associations, which also have to supply FDI and WHO with facts for a database for monitoring changes in oral health. To meet these important targets, it is necessary to have: the willing support of the Federation's national dental member associations: an FDI which includes most of the national dental associations in the world; and a continuation of the good cooperation with WHO and an acceptance by WHO that the FDI is a partner representing the absolute majority of the national dental associations in the world.316

Dentistry looks at adolescence during the 1980s

According to some, dentistry has followed suit with other health care factions by ignoring or misreading the oral health needs of adolescents.304 This is not to say that individualized care has not been good. The improving picture of oral health care in different countries over the last two decades suggests that children enter adulthood in better condition than did their parents. Whether this is due to our care of adolescents, or despite it remains to be demonstrated. Certain misconceptions and underrated factors to be examined below shape the dental image of the adolescent and may help to answer the above question.

First, adolescents are an ill-defined, de-emphasized group in the dental care system. At this writing, no textbook deals with the oral health needs of the adolescent as a specific entity. McDonald and Avery devote a chapter to adolescents in their widely used text, but the chapter focuses mainly on restorative needs and prosthetics. A monograph on adolescent dentistry, coined "ephebodontics" in the April 1969, issue of Dental Clinics of North America, is perhaps the most comprehensive text available, but it is 10 years old and it lacks current data and techniques in prevention, management, and behavior, to mention just a few areas.

At the professional level, activity has been scattered rather than coordinated. Efforts to eliminate junk foods from schools and the success of dental groups to make athletic mouthpieces mandatory are just two examples of the dental profession's recognition of the adolescent's special needs. The American Academy of Pedodontics' special committee appears to be an initial effort to begin to look at adolescence as a specific health care area. On the national level, one need only look at the tenor of health legislation aimed at the oral care of children.

Applewhite's304 excellent analysis of past programs portrays the approach to our youth's needs as well-intentioned and sound in principle but not carried to its logical end. Designers of these health programs presume that early childhood intervention prevents the development of costly restorative needs later in life. Unfortunately, practical obstacles prevent the realization of good oral health and oral health-seeking behavior.

As reported by Applewhite314, funding often stops during the elementary school years, so programs fall short of goals. Available money is spent treating primary teeth in the mixed dentition while it might be better spent on continued patient care during the teen years. It may also be a presumption that early treatment inculcates regular care-seeking behavior. Lambert and Freeman* show that children who were treated on an incremental basis in a clinical setting through the fourth grade had poorer oral health later on than did a similar group treated elsewhere.

These programs and the dental profession, in general, seem to have had little success in developing regular care-seeking behavior. If one looks at the two most prevalent oral health problems, caries, and periodontal disease, the adolescent period takes on greater significance as a critical period in a person's oral health life. Caries appears to be a major problem in adolescence, perhaps due to the eruption of the permanent teeth and the increase in proximal surfaces exposed to decay.

Massler's317 characterization of life in terms of caries experience reflects the risk of dental caries during adolescence (Fig. 2). The U.S. Public Health Service study 318 carried out during the late sixties supports Massler's projections for adolescents, but it adds some disheartening information to the oral health picture of the adolescent. The study of youths 12-17 years of age shows an increasing DMF rating through adolescence, levelling out in early adulthood. The study also points out that the DMF rating did not correlate significantly with race, education of parents, or family income, although "filled" teeth increased with family income.

The data indicate that caries is a problem that is

(1) widespread and

(2) not necessarily related to access to care, as suggested by the lack of relationship to parental income and education.

GreenbergTM319 presents some other views of the problem. Less than 4% of high school pupils are free of dental decay, and this same group averages two to three new lesions per person per year. A study by Dunning320 found that teenagers 16-18 years of age required 38% more dentist time per year mainly for operative care than did children 9-11 years of age.

These data all suggest that teenagers are not in a safe transitional period concerning dental caries. One must remember that

(1) these data are from 10- 20 years old, and that

(2) they do not account for the effects of more widespread fluoridation, the generalized acceptance of preventive dentistry, or the access to care created by third parties. Suomi T Mb 321 recently reviewed four decades of caries experience data for children and youths, but he was unable to make any conclusion about caries prevalence.

He did comment that few studies cover the last decade and that an estimation of the extent of caries among youths and children today is impossible. It seems we know very little about the caries picture of the adolescent. Brunswick and Nikias322 looked at inner-city teenagers' perceptions of oral health and found that although overall estimates of oral health by subjects agreed with those of dentists, the teenagers tended to overestimate their gingival health when compared to dentists' estimates using standard measures.

The problem is not confined to those with low socioeconomic status. Linn T M323 studied over 2000 predominantly white high school sophomores in the Midwest and found that although 94% had a regular dentist and 90% brushed daily, only a few (11%) flossed daily, and even fewer (1%) knew the full impact of dental plaque. Periodontal disease appears to have its genesis in adolescence and should not be thought of as an "adult disease," as it is often termed by the lay population and some professionals. The data on periodontal disease and oral health knowledge, caries, and care-seeking behavior highlight some of the problems of adolescence that are not fully understood or appreciated by the dental profession.

Also, problems related to malocclusion, dental phobias, traumatic injuries, management concerns, drug addiction, consent, and infectious disease present the dental practitioner with a complex patient who before adolescence was easily treated. Soft tissue changes in the oral cavity. Puberty gingivitis has been recognized by some and discounted by others as an identifiable entity. Baer324 considers the term a misnomer because it suggests that a hormonal imbalance is an etiologic agent; hormones may play a role but so, too, do local irritants.

The data on periodontal disease in adolescents, cited earlier, point to the genesis of gingival problems sometime in adolescence. Sutcliffe 325 in a longitudinal study of gingivitis and puberty in adolescents 11-17 years of age, found that gingivitis tended to peak and then to decline during the 6 years, and those peak periods of poor oral hygiene did not correlate significantly with peak periods of gingivitis. His data suggest a heightened tissue response.

The exact nature of the periodontal disease and its etiology in adolescence appears to be poorly understood. Other identifiable gingival problems associated with various stages of adolescence include acute necrotizing ulcerative gingivitis, infectious mononucleosis, periodontosis, recurrent apthous stomatitis, gingivitis associated with pregnancy. These problems can be related to the habits, emotional changes, and environment of the adolescent.

Oral Health goals vary from one country to the other and are restricted and very concise to the very population of the specific country based on their social, cultural, and environmental behaviors. Therefore, previous oral health goals for the Thai population were disease-based and typical of those set by many countries.

The oral health goals for adolescents in the year 2000 stated that not less than 75% of 18-year-olds should retain all 28 permanent teeth, and all 18-year-olds should have at least two sextants, on average, with healthy periodontal tissues (Community Periodontal Index; CPI = 0)12. In 2007, the Thai government published its oral health goals for 2020 following the FDI/WHO/IADR guidelines, and a theoretical framework for linking clinical status and quality of life was developed. The ultimate goal of the Thai Oral.

Dental Caries Drifting from the 1930s

New Zealand in the 1930s faced a very high prevalence of caries, particularly in children, and much edentulousness in adults of all ages. There was a very large unmet treatment requirement. This led to the development of two state-funded delivery systems: -for children by the School Dental Service, and -for adolescents by the Dental Benefit Scheme. The treatment of adults was provided in the private sector. A study in 1976 by Ross CB determined the standard of oral health and the treatment needs and examined public attitudes. Comparison with previous data showed a remarkable reduction in the prevalence of caries and the level of edentulousness.

Children and adolescents had little untreated decay (D = 1.3), few extractions, and large numbers of restored teeth (F = 11.9). Adults still had a high level of edentulousness. Generalized gingivitis was present in 6 percent of the young adult group and 20 percent of older adults. Polynesians, the lesser educated and low socio-economic groups had more periodontal disease at all ages. Two of the goals for the year 2000 should be achieved by 1988: i.e. 50 percent of 5- year-olds should be caries-free and 12-year-olds should have a DMFT of less than 3. Two more goals should be reached by the year 2000, i.e. 85 percent of those aged 18 should retain all their teeth and there should be a 50 percent reduction in edentulousness in the age group 34-44.326

Dental caries in the pediatric and adolescent population have continued to decline significantly over the past two decades, with approximately 50% of US schoolchildren considered to be caries-free. However, by the age of 17 years, only 15% of these young adults have not experienced caries. Over 85% of the lesions in the permanent dentition involve surfaces with pits and fissures, despite the availability of preventive measures such as sealants.

Of particular interest is the fact that 17% of children and adolescents account for 67% of the total caries experience. This distribution of dental caries demonstrates the need for a reliable screening method to determine those individuals at high-risk for caries development. The identification of these caries susceptible children and adolescents, and the development of innovative, caries-preventive protocols are necessary for further improvement in the oral health status of the pediatric age group and the creation of a caries-free population.327 The aim of this study conducted by Maria Gabriela Haye Biazevic et al. in the year 2008 was to assess oral health status and its relationship with quality of life.

Examinations were carried of which 45.75% were classified as belonging to socio-economic class C. Caries occurrence was observed in 218 subjects (88.26%); the mean DMFT was 5.40. The SiC index was 9.97. Almost half (47.77%) of the participants examined did not present sextants affected by periodontal disease. The following correlations were observed: a positive and statistically significant correlation between the highest score in the OHIP and decayed teeth; a positive correlation with threshold significance between OHIP and DMFT; an inverse correlation between intact teeth and OHIP; and a positive and non-statistically significant correlation between SiC and OHIP (correlation coefficient = 0.13, p = 0.245). 328

To effectively plan and implement oral-health education and treatment programs targeting school students, information on the social and behavioral correlations of caries and subsequent ailments is important. Such information is limited in developing countries in general and Tanzania in particular. This study by Mashoto and Kijakazi Obed in 2011 examined the prevalence of dental caries, its socio-behavioral distribution, and its impact on daily life activities in adolescents attending primary schools in Kilwa District, Tanzania. The crude prevalence of caries (DMFT>0) was 19.2% (20.4% weighted prevalence estimate).

The significant caries index (SiC), which gives the mean DMT of one-third of the most severely affected group, was 1.03. Thirty-six percent of adolescents (41.3% urban and 31.4% rural, p<0.001) reported at least one OIDP. Dental pain, dental caries, and oral problems impacted negatively on adolescents' daily performances.

Thus, the Child OIDP showed promising evaluative properties and responsiveness to change following treatment with ART fillings, extraction and OHE only. Results indicate that the Child OIDP inventory can detect the oral impact for school-going adolescents with pain-associated dental caries and is responsive to the change following treatment, particularly for tooth extraction. Developing policies targeting social and individual determinants of oral health is an urgent public-health strategy in Tanzania.329

This study by S. Krisdapong et al. in 2012 aimed to assess associations between sociodemographic and oral health behavioral factors with dental caries and oral health- related quality of life (OHRQoL) attributed to dental caries in a national representative sample of 12- and 15-year-old Thai children. Dental caries accounted for the significant associations of sugary snacks and drinks consumption with CS-impacts.

Significant associations of CS-impacts with consuming crispy snacks in 12-year-olds and fizzy drinks in 15-year-olds became non-significant when DT was entered into models. There were considerable geographic differences in DMFT and CS-impacts attributed to dental caries among Thai children.330 A study by K. P. Chakravathy et al. aimed to evaluate the relationship of body mass index (BMI) and dental caries with oral health-related quality of life (OHRQoL) among adolescents of Udupi district, India. Of 456 children, 34.4 % were overweight/obese.

There was a significant difference in the distribution of overweight/obese adolescents to age, gender, and frequency of sugar consumption. The prevalence of impacts ranged from 7.4–32.8 % in low normal and 12.9–49.7 % in overweight/obese adolescents. There was a significantly higher mean for overweight/obese than low normal adolescents for items related to "eating", "speaking", "sleeping", "smiling", "emotional status", OIDP total score, and caries. BMI and decayed teeth (DT) showed a significant association with the OIDP - Additive score. Adolescents with caries and increased BMI had poor OHRQoL.331

This study by Lee MO, Lee EJ aimed to examined the influence of socio-demographic, health-related, and oral health-related characteristics on adolescent DMFTs. DMFTs were smaller among boys than girls and smaller in the "13-15 age group" than in the "16-18 age group." In terms of household income, DMFTs were larger in the "lower," "lower-middle," and "upper-middle" income brackets than in the "upper" income bracket.

DMFTs were smaller among adolescents with a history of smoking than those who had never smoked. To improve the oral health of adolescents, oral health-promotion programs should be provided for girls, high school students, students from low-income families, smokers, and those who consider themselves to have poor oral health.332

According to Aguilar-Díaz et al, children with greater dental caries prevalence had higher scores for the following OHRQoL dimensions: oral symptoms, functional limitations, and emotional well-being. Adolescents reported a higher influence on functional limitations that involved difficulty in chewing firm foods and speaking.

These findings reinforce the fact that the influence on OHRQoL varies according to the participant's age group, as already described by Sheiham, Clementino et al, and Bekes et al.333 Rural, isolated areas benefit less from caries prevention programs and access to treatment than urban areas, and, hence, differences in oral health can be expected.

This study by Maria Cadenas de Llano-Pérula et al. in 2020 aims to assess the prevalence of caries and malocclusion in urban and rural areas of Peru and to compare them with patients' oral health perception. Significant differences in the prevalence ($p = 0.001$) and degree of caries ($p = 0.001$) were found between regions. The prevalence of caries was the highest in Cuzco (97.65%), followed by Titicaca (88.81%) and Lima (76.42%).

The severity of malocclusion was the lowest in Titicaca suggesting that higher the prevalence of caries and the more severe the malocclusion, the poorer the perception of oral health. In our study, rural areas presented a lower severity of malocclusion than urban areas.62 This study was carried out to measure the caries prevalence and treatment needs in school children of 6-14 year old residing in coastal areas of West Bengal.

Dental caries was founded low in the studied population. The overall all caries prevalence in the permanent dentition was 28.06%, in boys it was 25.39% and in girls, it was 30.86%. Therefore, caries prevalence in females was higher and was statistically highly significant ($P < 0.05$). The most frequently required treatment was one surface filling followed by other treatments irrespective of sex and age group. The presence of seafood containing high fluoride and the least availability of refined carbohydrates in the diet may be the reason for lower prevalence. 335

An epidemiological investigation was carried out to know the prevalence of Dental Caries amongst 1257 children attending schools in the city of Cuttack, Orissa. The point prevalence of dental caries was recorded to be 64.3% with an average DMFT of 2.38. The prevalence of caries showed a pattern of occurrence i.e. prevalence consistently increased from 5 years to 8 years age group and subsequently decreased at 11 years and 15 years age.

Regarding treatment needs, 63.6% of children required dental treatment for various reason and it is in accordance with dental caries prevalence of different age group.336

Malocclusion, Aesthetics and Perceived Orthodontics Treatment Needs

A cross-sectional study by C M de Oliveira and A Sheiham aimed to assess whether Brazilian adolescents who had completed orthodontic treatment had lower levels of impact on their oral health-related quality of life. Adolescents who had completed orthodontic treatment had fewer oral health-related impacts compared to the other two groups. They were 1.85 times (95% CI 1.30 to 2.62) less likely to have an oral health impact on their daily life activities than adolescents currently under treatment or 1.43 (1.01 to 2.02) times than those who never had treatment. Adolescents who had completed orthodontic treatment had a better oral health-related quality of life than those currently under treatment or those who never had treatment.337

A study by Eduardo Bernabé, Aubrey Sheiham & Cesar Messias de Oliveira aimed to assess the prevalence, intensity, and extent of the impacts on daily performances related to wearing different types of orthodontic appliances. The prevalence of condition-specific impacts related to wearing orthodontic appliances was 22.7%. Among adolescents with impacts related to wearing orthodontic appliances, 35.8% reported impacts of severe or very severe intensity, and 90.1% reported impacts on only one daily performance, commonly eating or speaking.

The prevalence, but not the intensity or the extent, of condition-specific impacts differed by type of orthodontic appliance (P = .001). One in four Brazilian adolescents undergoing orthodontic treatment reported side effects, specific impacts on daily living, related to wearing orthodontic appliances. Such impacts were higher among adolescents wearing fixed rather than removable or a combination of fixed and removable orthodontic appliances.338

A study was conducted by Mu Chen; Da-Wei Wang; Li-Ping Wu to determine changes in oral health-related quality of life (OHRQoL) during fixed orthodontic appliance therapy in Chinese patients. Patients were considerably compromised in terms of their overall OHRQoL until approximately 1 month after insertion. The severity of the compromised condition in terms of overall OHRQoL was greatest at 1 week with the reported impact on physical pain, psychological discomfort, and physical disability. Patients' OHRQoL was better after they completed the orthodontic treatment than before or during treatment.339 Malocclusion is a common oral disorder, can cause negative impacts on oral conditions, social life, and patients' self-confidence.

This study by N. Navabi et al. aimed to determine whether orthodontic treatment influences oral health-related quality of life (OHQoL). A significant relationship was found in one question and one domain of OHIP-14 between the two groups (P<0.05) which showed a difference in physical limitation. The linear regression model showed that in the treatment group, this domain of OHQoL was 1.86 times less likely complicated than in the "no treatment" group. Patients who had completed orthodontic treatment had a better OHQoL in physical aspects than those who never had treatment.340

A study by Daniela Feu et al. aimed to assess changes in oral health-related quality of life (OHQoL) in children undergoing fixed orthodontic treatment and compare it to that of two groups not receiving treatment. Two hundred eighty-four subjects aged 12-15 years were followed for 2 years; 87 were undergoing treatment at a university clinic (TG), 101 were waiting for treatment at this clinic (WG), and 96 were attending a public school and had never sought treatment (SG). OHQoL was assessed using the Oral Health Impact Profile (OHIP-14). All subjects were examined and interviewed at baseline (T1), 1 year later (T2), and 2 years later (T3). OHIP-14 scores were analyzed using negative binomial regression in generalized estimating equations for correlated data. During the follow-up period, the WG and TG OHIP-14 scores showed a statistically significant increase and decrease, respectively (P < .001).

At T1, the TG had an OHIP-14 score that was 1.9 times higher than that of the SG; however, at T3, the TG score was 60% lower than the initial score of the SG. Adjusting for age, gender, dental health status (DMFT), socioeconomic position, malocclusion severity, and self-perceived esthetics did not change the effect of orthodontic treatment on OHQoL. Fixed orthodontic treatment in Brazilian children resulted in significantly improved OHQoL after 2 years.341 De Oliveira and Sheiham conducted a cross-sectional study with 15- to 16-year-old Brazilian children and concluded that those who had completed orthodontic treatment had a better OHQoL than those currently undergoing treatment or those who had never been treated.

Chen et al. 339 followed 250 Chinese orthodontic patients and showed that their OHQoL was better after they completed treatment than before or during treatment. Nevertheless, one should be cautious when interpreting our results and not conclude that failure to obtain orthodontic treatment during adolescence may have a detrimental effect on QoL in adulthood, especially for those with mild or moderate orthodontic needs.342

To investigate the impact of wearing a fixed orthodontic appliance on oral health-related quality of life (OHRQoL) among adolescents. A case-control study (1-2) by Andréa A. Costa et al. was carried out with a population-based randomized sample of 327 adolescents aged 11 to 14 years enrolled at public and private schools in the City of Brumadinho, southeast of Brazil.

The case group (n = 109) was made up of adolescents with a high negative impact on OHRQoL, and the control group (n = 218) was made up of adolescents with a low negative impact. The outcome variable was the impact on OHRQoL measured by the Brazilian version of the Child Perceptions Questionnaire (CPQ11–14) – Impact Short Form (ISF:16).

The main independent variable was wearing fixed orthodontic appliances. Malocclusion and the type of school were identified as possible confounding variables. Bivariate and multiple conditional logistic regressions were employed in the statistical analysis. A multiple conditional logistic regression model demonstrated that adolescents wearing fixed orthodontic appliances had a 4.88-fold greater chance of presenting a high negative impact on OHRQoL (95% CI: 2.93–8.13; P < .001) than those who did not wear fixed orthodontic appliances.

A bivariate conditional logistic regression demonstrated that malocclusion was significantly associated with OHRQoL (P = .017), whereas no statistically significant association was found between the type of school and OHRQoL (P = .108). Adolescents who wore fixed orthodontic appliances had a greater chance of reporting a negative impact on OHRQoL than those who did not wear such appliances.343

Dental ailments like malocclusion affect not only the functional ability and aesthetic appearance of the person but also the psychological aspect of the individual. The study was aimed to find the relationship between quality of life and dental malocclusion among school-going adolescents in Tamil Nadu, India.

A cross-sectional study was conducted by A. Vinita Mary et al. among 342 subjects of the age range 14-19 years. The mean DMFT score was 1.86±2.77. A 203 (59.4%) did not require any orthodontic treatment while 139 (40.6%) had orthodontic treatment needs ranging from mild to very severe. It was seen that malocclusion affected some aspects of OHIP-14 significantly namely functional limitation, psychological discomfort, and psychological disability. The comparison of OHIP-14 scores between treatment needed and treatment not needed was highly significant (p<0.001).344

This was following a study conducted by Dash JK et al., among 15-year-old students and Joshi N et al., among 12-year-old children; where the prevalence of dental caries was found to be 62.2% and 77% respectively.336

The study conducted by Severine N. Anthony, Kayembe Zimba, and Balakrishnan Subramanian aimed to assess the prevalence of malocclusions and their impact on oral health-related quality of life (OHRQoL) among early adolescents in Ndola, Zambia. The overall reported impact on OHRQoL was 11.7%, which was significant (p<0.001) by age and sex, and higher in females than males. The overall prevalence of malocclusions was 27.9%, which was significant (p=0.005) by sex, and higher in males than females. Children with malocclusions reported significant (p<0.001) negative oral health impact compared to the children without malocclusions.

Spacing, diastema, and crowding were the most prevalent malocclusions that showed a clear inverse association with OHRQoL. The study findings provide indications that malocclusions are negatively associated with OHRQoL among early adolescents.345 Castro et al.346 reported that eating and cleaning mouth, which are the components of the Functional Well-Being domain in COHIP-SF19, had the highest impact on OHRQoL, and it supports the findings of this study on "difficulty in keeping teeth clean" but contrary to the findings on "difficulty in eating foods."

Oral Health-Related Quality of Life - Changing Trends

This study by Grath CM, Bedi R, Gilthorpe MS in March 2000 was designed to determine the United Kingdom public's perception of how oral health affects the quality of life (QoL) and to determine socio-demographic variations in these perceptions. 75% (1,340) believed their oral health either enhanced or reduced their QoL. Most frequently, this was perceived as being the result of its effect on eating. comfort and appearance. Other ways in which QoL was affected are also presented. Sociodemographic variations were apparent.

For example, people from higher socio-economic backgrounds believed that their oral health enhanced their QoL to a greater degree (OR=1.46, CI=1.20, 1.78) than the lower socio-economic groups. Women claimed that their oral health had a greater negative effect on QoL than did men (OR=1.36, CI=1.11, 1.64). Younger people (16-64 years old) reported that their oral health status reduced and enhanced QoL more than older adults (65 years and over) (OR=1.59, CI=1.23, 2.04). The study shows that the UK public perceives oral health as affecting their QoL in a variety of physical, social, and psychological ways and that significant socio-demographic variations exist in these observations.347

In a study conducted by Sudaduang Krisdapong, Aubrey Sheiham & Georgios Tsakos in 2009 aimed to assess the prevalence and characteristics of oral impacts on daily life, and the relationship between certain dental conditions and impacts attributed to them, in a nationally representative population of Thai school children aged 12 and 15 years. The three most commonly affected performances were eating (64.0%), cleaning teeth (55.3%), and maintaining an emotional state (53.1%). For both age groups, problems with gums were of less concern.

Oral impacts were common but not severe in Thai children and adolescents. For both age groups, impacts were mostly on eating performance; toothache and oral ulcers were the two important perceived causes reflecting needs for oral health promotion and treatment of dental caries and oral ulcers.348

Promoting the oral health of adolescents is important for the improvement of oral health globally. This study used baseline data from the LASH-project targeting secondary students to;

1) assess the frequency of poor oral hygiene status and oral impacts on daily performances, OIDP, by socio-demographic and behavioral characteristics,

2) examine whether socioeconomic and behavioral correlates of oral hygiene status and OIDP differed by gender and

3) examine whether the socio-demographic disparity in oral health was explained by oral health-related behaviors.

A Cross-sectional study was conducted in 2009 by Hawa S Mbawalla, Joyce R Masalu & Anne N Åstrom using a one-stage cluster sampling design. Older students, those from low socio-economic status families, had parents who couldn't afford dental care and had low educational-level reported oral impacts, poor oral hygiene, irregular toothbrushing, less dental attendance, and fewer intakes of sugar-sweetened drinks more frequently than their counterparts.

Behavioral factors accounted partly for the association between low family SES and OIDP. Low family SES, no dental attendance, and smoking experience were most important in males. Low family SES and fewer intakes of sugar-sweetened soft drinks were the most important correlates in females.349

Health Service is: "people of all ages should have oral health that enables good quality of life and social well-being" and clinical goals were set based on the assumption that a reduction in oral diseases would lead to a better quality of life. This study was aimed to assess the association between oral diseases and condition-specific oral health-related quality of life (CS-OHRQoL) as a basis for proposing OHRQoL-based goals for the population of 15-year-olds in Thailand.

Thirty-nine percent of 15-year-olds experienced moderate/higher levels of oral impacts on quality of life. Compared to those individuals with no tooth decay, adolescents with one or four or more decaying teeth were three and seven times more likely to experience moderate/higher impacts, respectively. Adolescents with extensive gingivitis in 3 or more mouth sextants were twice as likely to experience moderate/higher CS-impacts. Based on these findings, it is proposed that goals should focus on untreated decaying teeth and extensive gingivitis. Oral health goals for 15-year-olds should include specific OHRQoL measures.350

To evaluate the reliability and validity of an abbreviated version of the Oral Impact on Daily Performance (OIDP) questionnaire and to analyze the interrelationship between OIDP scores, socio-demographic characteristics, and oral health status among high school children in Davanagere city, Karnataka, India. This cross-sectional survey was conducted by GV Usha, HM Thippeswamy & L Nagesh among 900 school children aged between 12 and 15. Eating was the most common performance affected (33%) followed by cleaning teeth (22%) and speaking (20%). The severity of impacts was low for relaxing and carrying out works. The OIDP frequency score has acceptable psychometric properties in the context of an oral health survey among high school children of Davanagere city, Karnataka, India.351

Recent research has emphasized the relationships between environmental and individual factors that may influence population oral health and lead to health inequalities. However, little is known about the effect of interactions between environmental and individual factors on inequalities in clinical (e.g., decayed teeth) and subjective oral health outcomes (e.g., oral health-related quality of life [OHQoL]).

This cohort study conducted by E Gupta et al. in 2015 aimed to explore the direct and mediated longitudinal interrelationships between key environmental and individual factors on clinical and subjective oral health outcomes in adults. Accordingly, the present findings and the adapted Wilson and Cleary/Brunner and Marmot model on which they are predicted provide support for the psychosocial pathway being key in the SES–oral health relationship.

The pathways through which environmental factors interact with individual factors to impact subjective oral health outcomes identified here may bring opportunities for more targeted oral health promotion strategies.352 Oral health status and oral health-related quality of life (OHRQoL) of working adolescents have been very little reported in the literature.

Therefore, this study by Sultan Keles, Filiz Abacigil, and Filiz Adana aimed to determine oral health status and OHRQoL in a group of adolescent workers. The results showed significant relationships between the tooth brushing frequency, dental visit frequency, dental trauma history, smoking, and the OHIP-14 subdomains ($p < 0.05$). Poor oral health and a lack of good oral health attitudes may harm the oral health-related quality of life (OHRQoL) of working adolescents.

Dental health education programs in collaboration with schools and dental health services may be beneficial for promoting oral health and improving the OHRQoL of working adolescents.353 El-Kalla et al. reported that dental trauma has a negative impact on the quality of life regarding social, functional, and emotional aspects if left unrestored.354 Following their study, we found that teeth broken due to trauma in the anterior region, which were left untreated, affected the OHRQoL of our participants.

Soares et al stated that enamel fracture had no significant impact on children' quality of life, while enamel-dentin fracture did have an impact on the quality of life.355 In previous studies concerning the prevalence of caries in Albania, Hysi 47 in 12-year-old students reported a value of 3.8 whereas Laganà 356 reported that in 7-15-year-old students, the value was only 2.3. On the other hand, Thelen 357 in a similar sample (16- 19-year-old students) evaluated the DMTF value to be 4.6. In Albania during the period 1990-2007, DMFT increased from 2.8 to 3.8.

This tendency could be explained by better clinical examinations of dental conditions, which were absent or incomplete in the past. The socioeconomic status of patients seeking orthodontic treatment is important in a developing country like India. No public funding is available at a large scale for the treatment of malocclusion.

This study aimed to test the null hypothesis that there is no influence of socioeconomic status and family type on oral health-related quality of life (OHRQoL) among adolescents in central Kerala

There was a significant association between the socioeconomic status of the individuals and OHRQoL at both bivariate and multivariate analyses. The family type also showed a significant relation at the bivariate level. The null hypothesis that there is no influence of socioeconomic status and family type on OHRQoL was rejected.358 Dental diseases negatively influence people's oral health-related quality of life (OHRQoL) and thus their perceived need for dental care. QoL is increasingly acknowledged as a valid, appropriate and significant indicator of service need and intervention outcomes in contemporary public health research and practice.

The study by Sudhanshu Sanadhya et al. aimed to assess the psychometric properties of oral health impact profile-14 (OHIP-14) scale among rural and urban OHIP of the Udaipur population & to assess and compare clinical dental status (dental caries, periodontal disease, and prosthetic status) and its impacts on OHRQoL rural and urban population of Udaipur.

Prevalence of periodontal disease (community periodontal index and loss of attachment) was found greater among the rural population than the urban population. The urban population showed a significantly greater proportion of subjects with prosthesis (including partial, fixed, and total) as compared to the rural population.

Among the study population, OHIP-14 was significantly ($P \leq 0.05$) associated with age, gender, presence of decayed teeth (DT), missing teeth (MT), and location. The rural and urban study subjects had a fair clinical status. The presence of dental caries had greatest impacts on OHRQoL. In addition, rural subjects faced greater impact than urban subjects.359

Kids and teenagers are more prone to oral diseases. Poor oral health has a significant impact on oral well-being–associated quality of life. Thus, an investigation by Neeta Sinha et al. was performed to examine the outcome of oral health status on the quality of life of children and adolescents in the Indian population, by using the Oral Health Impact Profile-14 (OHIP-14).

The results showed a statistically noteworthy association between the toothbrushing regularity, the number of dental appointments, history of oral trauma, smoking, and subdomains of OHIP-14 ($P < 0.05$). The dental and oral health of an individual has a great impact on their quality of life.360

Gingivitis, and Periodontal Health

Optimal oral hygiene practices are instrumental to achieving good dental and gingival health. The purpose of this study by Clement Chinedu Azodo & Ashu Michael Agbor was to determine the gingival health and oral hygiene practices of schoolchildren in the North West region of Cameroon. Out of 2287 school children examined, 1676 (73.3 %) had normal gingiva while 26.7 % had gingivitis of varying severity.

Gingivitis was found significantly more in rural dwellers ($P = 0.001$). In terms of the severity of the recorded gingivitis, mild gingivitis constituted 549 (89.9 %), moderate gingivitis 49 (8.0 %), and severe gingivitis 13 (2.1 %). The majority-1929 (85.4 %) of the participants had received instruction on how to care for their teeth and the predominant source of this instruction was from their parents. Irregular teeth cleaning was marked 1137 (49.7 %) among the children. 361

Gingivitis is a common oral health problem. Untreated gingivitis may progress to periodontitis, a common cause of tooth loss. The prevalence of gingivitis and calculus among Puerto Rican children is unknown. Understanding this prevalence can support early public health preventative strategies. This study conducted by Augusto R. Elias-Boneta et al. aimed to estimate the prevalence of gingivitis and calculus among 12- year-old Puerto Ricans by health region and to explore differences in distribution by school type (a proxy for socio-economic status) and gender.

Gingivitis was found in 80.41% of the 1586 children evaluated. Urban-public schoolchildren had a slightly higher prevalence (83.24%) compared to private (79.15%, $p = 0.16$); those in rural-public (77.59%) and private schools had similar prevalence ($p = 0.15$). Extensive gingivitis was present in 60.81% of all children. The mean percentage of sites presenting BOP (BOP%) was 17.79%. Rural and urban public schoolchildren presented significantly higher BOP% compared to children from private schools ($p = 0.0005$, $p = 0.002$, respectively). Dental calculus was detected in 61.59% of the sample, boys presenting significantly higher ($p = 0.005$) total and supragingival calculus. Rural-public schoolchildren had a significantly higher prevalence of subgingival calculus compared to private schoolchildren ($p = 0.02$).

Gingivitis prevalence is higher among 12-year-old Puerto Ricans compared to data reported for U.S. adolescents. Public schoolchildren presented significantly higher BOP% sites compared to private schoolchildren. Boys presented a significantly higher total and supragingival calculus prevalence than girls. Oral health disparities related to gender and school type were identified by this study. Studies exploring the reasons for these disparities are recommended.362

A study by SG Gökalp et al. aimed to estimate the severity of dental caries and the periodontal status of children and adults in Turkey. Only 30.2% of the 5-year-old group was caries-free, and the mean dmft was 3.7. Mean DMFT was 1.9 in 12- year-olds, 2.3 in 15-year-olds, 10.8 in 35-44-year-olds, and 25.8 in 65-74-year-olds. In both adolescents and adults, the prevalence of caries was higher among females than in males.

In rural areas, the prevalence of caries was high among 5-year-olds, while DMFT was high in the elderly. The prevalence of dental caries was similar for 12- and 15-year-olds in urban and rural areas. Healthy periodontal tissue was noted in 56.2% of fifteen-year-olds.363 The need for treatment of destructive periodontal diseases is based on observations made by oral health professionals, who, prompted by clinical findings, recommend treatment.

We hypothesized that clinical signs of periodontal destruction have an impact on the oral-health-related quality of life of adolescents. A cross-sectional study among 9203 Chilean high school students. The results showed that both attachment loss [OR = 2.0] and necrotizing ulcerative gingivitis [OR = 1.6] were significantly associated with higher impact on the Oral Health-Related Quality of Life of adolescents. Individuals in lower socioeconomic positions systematically reported a higher impact on their oral-health-related quality of life.364

To assess whether gender and age differences can be found in different aspects of health-related quality of life (HRQOL) of children and adolescents, and to what extent these results correspond to theoretical and empirical findings from developmental psychology.

Children report a very good quality of life largely independent of gender. After 12 years, HRQOL decreases in the majority of aspects. In the physical and psychological dimensions, a stronger decrease is found for females than for males. Children have higher HRQOL than adolescents in many aspects. With increasing age, HRQOL is frequently worse for females than for males. Examination of the individual aspects leads to a differentiation of the results with relevance for public health.365

Socioeconomic Status

There is an increasing recognition that children's oral health-related quality of life (OHRQoL) is affected by social and environmental factors. The study was conducted by Nikhil Ahuja and Nirmala Ahuja aimed to assess the influence of socioeconomic status and home environment factors on OHRQoL among 13–14-year-old schoolchildren in North Bengaluru.

In both government and private schools, mean CPQ11-14 scores were highest for children belonging to upper lower class followed by the lower middle, upper middle, and upper class of socioeconomic status, showing statistically significant differences ($P < 0.05$). In government schools, children living with single parent/guardian, having two or more siblings, one or two rooms, staying with more than one person per room, family using alcohol/tobacco reported higher mean CPQ11-14 scores as compared to private schools. ($P < 0.05$). 366 Besides, children who occupy socioeconomically lower positions are more likely to engage in unhealthy oral health behaviors including dietary choices and access to dental care.

Furthermore, due to poverty, they lack the necessary economic or educational resources for health promotion initiatives and suffer from psychological and social problems. It is therefore important to understand the existence of this social gradient and take effective action to tackle these oral health inequalities.367 A study by São Lourenço da Mata - PE, Brazil aimed to identify the sociodemographic factors and the oral health conditions related to the impact on the quality of life of adolescents. High impact on oral health-related quality of life was evidenced in 66.1% of adolescents. The prevalence of dental caries, gingival bleeding, and pain were respectively 51.29%, 49.60%, and 73.6%.

The multiple regression analysis found that the high impact on the quality of life was related to the oral health condition and sex of teenagers, showing that girls, who had a higher prevalence of dental caries and pain, had a greater impact related to oral health. Dental caries and pain of dental origin cause a high impact on the quality of life of adolescents, being higher among girls.368 A study conducted by Seham Mohamed and Mario V. Vettore aimed to evaluate whether socioeconomic position exerts a mediating and/or moderating effect on the association between oral clinical measures and oral health-related quality of life (OHRQoL) in adolescents.

The impact of all oral clinical conditions on adolescents' OHRQoL was lower in the low-family-income groups compared with those with a better income. Socioeconomic position partially mediated the relationship between the four oral clinical measures and OHRQoL. Sobel's test confirmed these findings ($P < 0.001$).

The findings suggest the importance of the socioeconomic position as a moderator and mediator factor between oral clinical measures and OHRQoL. Disadvantaged adolescents are likely to experience poor OHRQoL due to oral conditions. The reduction of the impact of oral conditions on quality of life in adolescents may be enhanced by addressing social inequalities related to oral health.369 Socioeconomic inequalities are recognized as a major problem with people in low socioeconomic groups having worse subjective oral health outcomes, including oral health-related quality of life (OHRQoL).

However, only a few longitudinal studies assessed the impact of contextual and individual socioeconomic determinants in adolescents' OHRQoL. Camila S. Sfreddo estimated the impact of socioeconomic inequalities on adolescents' OHRQoL over 2 years. Adolescents with lower mean income in school neighborhoods ($P < 0.05$), household income ($P < 0.05$), and maternal schooling ($P < 0.05$) had higher overall CPQ11-14 scores. Female sex, attending a dentist by toothache, dental caries, and malocclusion were also associated with higher overall CPQ11-14 scores. Adolescents from low socioeconomic backgrounds reported worse OHRQoL at 2-year follow-up compared to those from high socioeconomic backgrounds. Actions toward health inequalities need to address socioeconomic factors in adolescence.370

This study aimed to assess caries prevalence and experience among 11 to 14 years, school children, analyze demographic, socioeconomic, personal, and professional dental care to untreated carious lesions, and evaluates the effect of decayed teeth on early adolescents' oral health-related quality of life (OHRQoL). The average scores of DMFT and DT in this study were 2.97 ± 1.29 and 1.66 ± 1.24. Poisson regression analysis demonstrated that early adolescents whose mothers with a lower level of education and of low socioeconomic status were 1.41 and 1.27 times respectively had higher DT scores when compared with their peers.

Untreated cavities are affected mainly by mother education, school type, family income, and regular dental appointments. Children with DMFT≤3) or DT = 0 recorded a statistically significant lower CPQ11–14 average score ($p<0.01$) and ($p<0.0001$) respectively. Untreated carious cavities and caries experience were associated with lower socioeconomic, maternal education, and less frequent tooth brushing. Untreated carious cavities have a significant negative impact on schoolchildren's QoL.371 There is a lack of studies considering the social disparity in oral health emanating from adolescents in low-income countries.

This study by Kijakazi O Mashoto et al. aimed to assess socio-demographic disparities in clinical- and self-reported oral health status and several oral health behaviors. The extent to which oral health-related behaviors might account for socio-demographic disparities in oral health status was also examined. The majority of students were caries-free (79.8%) and presented with a low need for dental treatment (89.3%).

Compared to their counterparts in opposite groups, rural residents and those from less poor households presented more frequently with caries experience (DMT>0), high need for dental treatment, and poor oral hygiene behavior, but were less likely to report poor oral health status. Stepwise logistic regressions revealed that social and behavioral variables varied systematically with caries experience, high need for dental treatment, and poor self-reported oral health.

Socio-demographic disparities in oral health outcomes persisted after adjusting for oral health behaviors.329

THIRTEEN

Trends in Adolescents

Throughout the world, interest in adolescents' issues over the past decade has increased, as reflected by various global activities, such as the International Youth Year in 1985 and the 1989 technical discussions of the World Health Organization, the topic of which was the health of youth. In December 2009, the United Nations General Assembly adopted a resolution proclaiming the year commencing 12 August 2010 as the International Year of Youth. The resolution calls upon governments, civil society, individuals, and communities worldwide to support activities at local and international levels to mark the event. Reasons for this rising interest include an increased focus on education and concern about industrialization and urbanization of developing countries, which has a disproportionate impact on young people.

These trends bring with them situations previously unknown in the developing world: delayed marriages, out-of-wedlock births, unemployment, and substance abuse. The consequence is that, increasingly, the health problems of youth in developing nations are parallel to those of the industrialized world, with both the opportunities and challenges that comparison implies. Adolescence and young adulthood are unique periods in the life span that present opportunities and challenges in improving health. The life course health development framework recognizes that many influences shape health and views health status as a trajectory, with early events and influences shaping later outcomes. 372 Transitional periods, when individuals are more sensitive to environmental inputs, assume a critical role in this framework.

Adolescence and young adulthood involve significant growth and development. During adolescence, young people are increasingly independent, taking greater responsibility for habits in areas including diet and exercise. Many initiate adult behaviors in areas including driving, substance use, and sexual activity.378 These habits and behaviors influence health in the short and long term. Experimentation with adult behavior reflects normative development; however, early initiation of normative adult behavior or the initiation of health-damaging behaviors is of concern. Young adulthood also entails significant transition. This period may involve many paths—such as college, military, employment—and each has implications for health status and access to care. Many traditional markers of adolescent health—including rates of homicide, unintentional injury, substance use, drinking and driving, and sexually transmitted infections (STIs)—peak during this period.

As they acquire the rights and privileges of adulthood, young adults lose support from institutions and safety net programs that serve adolescents. Many navigate this transition successfully, but those who rely heavily on institutional support face a greater risk of poor outcomes. Although multiple national, research, policy, and program initiatives have addressed adolescent health, we know little about improving young adult health or developing systems to serve this population. 373-375 The study done by Guy S. Parcel, Philip R. Nader, and Michael P. Meyer in 1977, is presented as a model for the needs assessment phase of planning and delivering adolescent health care and health education services for a community. The highest- ranked concerns and problems were school, drugs, sex, getting along with parents and adults, acne, depression, and overweight.

Ninety-one percent reported they often or sometimes worry about their health. Sources of medical care were family physicians (56.8%) and hospital emergency rooms (15.9%). Reported visits in the past year were none (27.5%); one (24.1%); two to three (32.2%); and four or more (14.7%).373 In analyzing responses according to sex, grade, and ethnic background, several implications are apparent: (1) many of the concerns and problems identified require educational as well as health care services; (2) the diverse perceived health needs of an entire high school population indicate that the traditional one-semester general health course for all is grossly inadequate; and (3) students' concerns and problems are not limited to the areas of drugs, venereal disease, and unwanted pregnancy. The report gives findings from five nationally representative surveys of high school seniors from 1975 through 1979 to examine the correlates of licit and illicit drug use and to consider whether recent changes in youthful drug use are linked to any changes in the correlates.

Males still exceed females in the use of alcohol and marijuana, but no longer in cigarette smoking. Black seniors now report less drug use than Whites. Other dimensions of family background, region, and urbanicity show only modest associations with drug use. Above-average drug use occurs among those less successful in adaptation to the educational environment, as indicated by truancy and low grades; those who spend many evenings out for recreation; and those with heavy time commitments to a job and/or relatively high incomes. Drug use is below average among seniors with strong religious commitments and conservative political views. From 1975 through 1979, among senior's cigarette use peaked and subsequently declined, marijuana use rose and then levelled off, and the (still infrequent) use of cocaine rose rapidly. However, these shifts in drug use were not accompanied by substantial shifts in the above correlates of use.

The findings thus suggest that the kinds of young people most at risk remain much the same, while the types and amounts of substances they use shift somewhat from year to year. 376 An investigation of trends in dental caries in the Australian adolescent population was possible through the development of a predictive model for caries severity. Past associations of predictor variables with caries severity were separated from a wide range of ad hoc surveys, clinical trials, and analyses of service records. National trends in the identified predictor variables were then used to predict past and future caries severity for the Australian adolescent population. Caries severity marginally decreased between 1965 to 1970. Over the period 1970 to 1980 caries severity markedly decreased. Caries severity was predicted to continue to decrease over the period 1980 to 1990, but with evidence of a plateauing for younger adolescents by 1990.

Marked increases in percentages of younger adolescents caries-free between 1975 and 1990 were also predicted. The predictions appeared to be tracking adequately with subsequently available data. 377 A pilot survey of oral health done by R. G. Schamschula et al. in the year 1980 stated that dental caries prevalence (mean DIMFT per person) increased from 17.1 at 20 years to 20.7 at 35 years and declined to 14.6 by the age of 50 years and over. Oral hygiene (OHI) was poor overall and deteriorated with age. Periodontal status (PI) was significantly correlated with the presence of debris (DI) and calculus (CI). Tooth mortality reached 75% by the age of 43 years. Prosthetic needs were correspondingly high, but 95% of denture requirements were unmet. No evidence of effective or sustained oral health care was seen; 38% of subjects needed emergency treatment.374 This study is part of the Cross-National Survey on Health Behaviour in Schoolchildren- -A WHO Collaborative Study, which started in 1982 aimed to describe the oral health habits (oral hygiene habits, use of sugar snacks, and use of fluorides) in schoolchildren in 11 countries.

Toothbrushing was consistently less frequent among boys than among girls. The use of dental floss is still very rare. Efforts must be continued to reduce the consumption of sweets and soft drinks. These findings should be taken into consideration when attempts are made to improve oral health education. 379 This 5-year longitudinal study monitored 167 subjects at ages 14.3, 16.0, and 19.6 years. The aims were (1) to determine loss of attachment ≥ 1 mm in the study group over the 5 years; (2) to relate baseline levels of oral deposits and gingivitis to the 5-year increment of loss of attachment; (3) to determine whether subjects who had developed loss of attachment ≥ 1 mm by age 16 years were more susceptible to further development of loss of attachment; (4) to evaluate the loss of attachment indices. Loss of attachment, plaque, subgingival calculus, gingival bleeding, and gingival color change was measured. At baseline, 3% of subjects had loss of attachment ≥ 1 mm, and < 1% of sites were involved. By age 19 years, 77% had loss of attachment ≥ 1 mm, and 31% of sites were affected.

There was a significant correlation between the presence of subgingival calculus at baseline and the 5-year increment of loss of attachment (Pearson's $r = 0.26$ $p < 0.001$). Subjects who had developed loss of attachment by age 16 years still had significantly more sites affected at the more severe 2 mm level 3 years later than their peers ($p < 0.05$).

The results suggest that a flexible approach is needed in selecting indices of loss of attachment for epidemiological investigations. 380 This study investigated the occurrence of caries among 15-year-olds using the municipal oral health service in Helsinki in 1976 and 1986. Data were collected from each subject's dental health file as recorded during routine check-ups by dentists in the health center of the city of Helsinki in the year in question.

All indicators showed a significant improvement (p < 0.001) in dental health during the 10 years. The percentage of intact teeth and surfaces increased markedly. The mean number of DMF teeth per person fell from 12.1 to 5.1 and that of proximal DF surfaces from 5.6 to 1.5. In the 1976 group, 63% of all occlusal surfaces had been filled or were decayed. Ten years later the figure was 26%. Proximal DFS percentages were 10 and 3%, respectively. The ratios of the total number of proximal to occlusal DFS were 0.6 in 1976 and 0.4 in 1986. 381 A cross-sectional study by Freire M, Hardy R, and Sheiham A aimed to investigate the relationship between mothers' sense of coherence (SOC) and their adolescent children's oral health. SOC is the central construct of the salutogenesis model of health, which seeks to explain factors that promote health.

Two sets of outcome variables were selected for the analyses: oral health status (dental caries, oral cleanliness, and periodontal disease), and oral health-related behaviors (daily frequency of sugar intake, toothbrushing frequency, and pattern of dental attendance). Adolescents whose mothers had higher levels of SOC score had lower levels of dental caries and gingival bleeding after probing and were less likely to visit the dentist mainly when in trouble than those whose mothers had lower levels of SOC. Mothers' SOC was associated with their children's levels of dental caries and periodontal disease, as well as a pattern of dental attendance. Interventions designed to improve or maintain the oral health of young people should take into consideration the family environment.375 A study was conducted by Fitzgerald RP et al. in September 2004 to investigate adolescents' views of oral health and oral health care, to increase understanding of the influences on their use or non-use of free care. While aware of the normative pressure to attend for free dental care and engage in oral health care, adolescents consider doing so to be "just so gay". They exhibit strongly held preconceptions about the expense of dentistry and the respective competence of dentists and dental therapists.

The dental surgery environment was viewed as a major disincentive. Adolescent oral health beliefs centered on two models: the medicalized, pragmatic view of oral health (which valued the function of teeth); and the cosmetic view of oral health (which valued the aesthetics of teeth); or a combination of these two models. In both models, media advertising for oral health care products was a significant source of oral health information. The preferred oral health behavior associated with the medicalized model was the frequent use of chewing gum and rapid toothbrushing, and, for the cosmetic model frequent use of chewing gum and breath fresheners. These findings support the international literature on the use/non-use of dental services even when the financial barriers to seeking such services have been removed. 382 The wearing of dental "grills" in the mouths of children, adolescents, and adults is a problematic fad currently facing the dental community.

A grill is a gold, platinum, or other metal and often jewel-encrusted encasement for the dentition. The grill can be easily placed over the existing teeth and is fabricated by simply obtaining an impression of an area of a person's mouth over which a grill is desired. The study by Hollowell, William H aimed to report the oral and dental manifestations of a case in which a grill was worn by an uninformed adolescent consumer. A 16-year-old African American male was clinically evaluated on a routine recall appointment in this case. He had evidence of new rampant anterior decay in an oral cavity that had previously been caries-free on all earlier regular hygiene visits. A strong factor contributing to decay was the purchase and regular wear of a grill from a neighborhood jewelry store.

This case report was conducted to alert dental professionals, more specifically pediatric dentists, about the increased popularity of the grill and the detrimental effects that it can have upon unhygienic dentition.383 A study was conducted by Karen G Peres et al in 2009 to estimate the prevalence of oral health impacts and its association with life course socioeconomic variables, dental status, and dental services utilization in a population-based birth cohort in Southern Brazil. The response rate was 94.4% (n = 339). The prevalence of OIDP = 1 was 30.1% (CI95%25.2;35.0) and OIDP ≥ 2 was 28.0% (CI95%23.2;32.8). The most common daily activity affected was eating (44.8%), followed by cleaning the mouth and smiling (15.6%, and 15.0%, respectively). In the final model, mother schooling and mother employment status in early cohort participant's life was associated with OIDP in adolescence. As higher untreated dental caries at age 6 and 12 years, and the presence of dental pain, gingival bleeding, and incisal crowing in adolescence as higher the OIDP score.

On the other hand, dental fluorosis was associated with a low OIDP score. Our findings highlight the importance of adolescent's early life social-environmental as mother schooling and mother employment status and the early and later dental status on the adolescent's quality of life regardless of family income and use of dental services.384 The aim of this epidemiological survey by Ostberg AL et al. in 2010 was to describe and analyze oral health habits and lifestyle factors concerning the priority of regular dental care in 19-year-old individuals with specific reference to gender, residential area, and socioeconomic grouping.

The analysis revealed that males had significantly less favorable oral health habits than females. 41% of the males and 30% of the females did not plan regular dental visits after the age of 20 when they will be charged for the care ($p = 0.002$). There were no statistically significant differences in oral health habits and dental care priorities in residential areas and socio-economic groups. In a multivariate model, three significant factors for the probability of "not planning for future regular dental visits" were identified: toothbrushing less than twice daily (OR 1.94; 95% CI 1.28-2.94), smoking (OR 1.68; 95% CI 1.10-2.56) and male gender (OR 1.54; 95% CI 1.05-2.24). The findings emphasize the need for the promotion of favorable oral health habits and smoking prevention among adolescents. There is also a need for dental personnel to recognize differences in oral health-related attitudes and behaviors between males and females.385 The aim of the study conducted by Jessica S. Ericsson et al. in 2012 was to analyze oral health-related perceptions, attitudes, and behavior to oral hygiene conditions. Higher scores of plaque and gingivitis were significantly related to the following perceptions:

(i) a less favorable oral health situation,

(ii) lower satisfaction with the aesthetic appearance of the teeth,

(iii) more frequent gingival bleeding during toothbrushing,

(iv) less favorable self-care of the teeth,

(v) a lower possibility to impact on own oral health,

(vi) lower importance of cleaning the teeth, and

(vii) lower importance of good oral health conditions.

More favorable oral hygiene conditions and more positive perceptions, attitudes, and behaviors towards oral health were found among female subjects than among male subjects. In conclusion, adolescents with high scores of plaque and gingivitis had less positive perceptions, attitudes, and behaviors towards oral health than those with more favorable oral hygiene conditions.386 To elicit perceptions of oral health in children and adolescents as an initial step in the development of oral health item banks for the Patient-Reported Oral Health Outcomes Measurement Information System project. Carl A. Maida et al. in 2015 conducted focus groups with ethnically, socioeconomically, and geographically diverse youth (8–12, 13–17 years) to identify perceptions of oral health status. They identified three unique themes that the youth associated with their oral health status:

(1) understanding the value of maintaining good oral health over the life course, for longevity and quality of life in the adult years;

(2) positive association between maintaining good oral health and interpersonal relationships at school, and dating, for older youth; and

(3) knowledge of the benefits of orthodontic treatment to appearance and positive self-image while holding a strong view as to the discomfort associated with braces.

The results provide valuable information about core domains for the oral health item banks to be developed and generated content for new items to be developed and evaluated with cognitive interviews and in a field test.387

Eating disorders are among the most prevalent disorders in adolescence and can have negative consequences including poor quality of life, medical complications, and even death. This study conducted by Mark S. Allen, Davina A. Robson, and Sylvain Laborde provide evidence that normal variations in personality are related to eating behavior, oral health, and eating disorder symptoms during mid-adolescence.388 Worldwide estimates of childhood obesity are as high as 43 million, and rates continue to increase each year.

Childhood obesity is a growing problem in the present era and it causes serious consequences in the later years. In today's society, electronic media have been thoroughly integrated into the fabric of life, with television, video games, and computers being central to both work and play. While these media outlets can provide education and entertainment to children, many researchers are concerned with the negative impact of electronic media on children.

The study conducted by Nithya Anand,M. Suresh, and S.C. Chandrasekaran aimed to evaluate the correlation, to how oral hygiene and periodontal health were influenced by obesity and lifestyle factors, The prevalence of poor oral hygiene and poor dietary habits were observed in children who spent more time watching television, playing videogames, and using the computer. Good oral hygiene was observed in children who had visited dentists in the past. There is a strong association of lifestyle factors with oral hygiene in children. A sedentary lifestyle, with more leisure activities, negatively impacts the oral health of children.389

Adolescents and Smoking

Tobacco smoking is thought to be responsible for more than 1 million premature deaths annually worldwide.390 The Surgeon General has labeled smoking as the chief single avoidable cause of death in the United States and the most important public health risk.391 Numerous studies have shown that adolescents are the group most at risk for beginning to smoke392 and that smoking in early adolescence is a strong predictor of smoking in adulthood. 390,391,393,395 Smoking is also a predictor of other dangerous behaviors of late adolescence, such as substance abuse, alcohol abuse, promiscuity, and reckless driving.391,396 Kandel and Yamaguchi 392 found that the risk of initiating smoking increases steadily from age 12 to 16 years and then begins to decline.

The matter is largely settled by the age of 20 years. If a person is still a nonsmoker at this age, he or she is unlikely to begin.390 Thus, the most important public health issue of this era and the single most avoidable cause of death hinges on adolescent smoking prevention and cessation. Although numerous studies have related both sociodemographic and psychosocial factors to adolescent smoking, much remains to be learned about causal relationships.

While the CASS study397 identified factors that are predictive of smoking onset and need to be targeted for interventions, practical methods must be sought in working with adolescents to achieve this goal. Current school-based smoking prevention programs for adolescents appear to have a significant impact on the prevention of smoking initiation,398 but as yet none has reported a decrease among regular smokers, and follow-up is not sufficiently long to determine whether regular smoking has been deterred.398

This lack of impact on smoking adolescents may be a result of the prevailing influence of smoking behavior among peers. Peer relations are important socializing processes for many health behaviors 399,400 and adolescence marks a particularly vulnerable developmental stage for social influences.401 Also, developmental theories 402 suggest that the socio-contextual environment shapes adolescent development, such that there is a continuous, bidirectional interaction between individual characteristics and socio-contextual factors.

Adolescent friendships are one of the most salient relationships during adolescence and are thus uniquely situated to impact adolescent health behavior. Although a myriad of factors contributes to adolescent smoking, previous research has consistently demonstrated that adolescents are influenced by the cigarette use of their friends. 403 Adolescents have been shown to form friendships based around shared smoking habits 404 and alter their smoking based on their friends' actual or perceived smoking patterns. However, it is also known that some substances are perceived as more socially acceptable, particularly during adolescence.405

Cigarette smoking, specifically, has shown overall declines in social acceptability in recent decades.406 Besides, low levels of perceived social acceptability of smoking have been shown to predict success in smoking cessation interventions for adolescents. Further, perceived sibling approval of smoking is associated with future smoking in adolescents. 26 Yet, no research to date has considered the role of perceived acceptability of smoking when examining social influence from friends on cigarette smoking.

Knowledge regarding health risks does not seem to deter adolescents from smoking. In one study, 90% of adolescents were aware that smoking was a health hazard, but few believed that smoking was a threat to their health.2 Understanding why adolescents begin and continue to smoke is critical and may lead to effective preventive and cessation techniques that have thus far remained elusive

FOURTEEN
DISCUSSION

Perhaps the easiest concept to define is subjective oral health. We would suggest that this refers to the functional and psychosocial impacts of oral diseases and conditions as perceived by the individual. While current measures assess the frequency with which these impacts occur, they fail to establish the meaning and significance of those impacts to the individuals who complete the questionnaires, particularly with respect to their effects on perceptions of quality of life.

Consequently, we would define OH-QoL as the impact of oral disorders on aspects of everyday life that are important to patients and persons, with those impacts being of sufficient magnitude, whether in terms of severity, frequency or duration, to affect an individual's perception of their life overall. The World Health Organization Quality of Life (WHOQOL) Group defined quality of life as 'the individual's perception of their position in life in the context of the culture and value systems in which they live and in relation to their goals, expectations, standards and concerns'. 408 This suggests that quality of life is a complex multidimensional phenomenon that is not captured solely by questions about health.

Fitzpatrick et al. 409 presumed that the use of the term quality of life is 'unhelpful' since it 'misleadingly suggests an abstract or philosophical set of judgments or issues relating to life in the broadest sense of factors outside the person, such as living standards, political or physical environments'. Moreover: 'Because, of the vast array of so-called quality of life measures used in health settings, we avoid using this terminology as much as possible'. 409 Accordingly, they suggest that 'patient-based outcome measures' rather than 'quality of life measures' be used as a collective term for instruments that assess perceptions of health, its consequences and the benefits derived from therapeutic interventions.

Leplege and Hunt 410 also suggest that the notion of quality of life, even when health-related, should be abandoned altogether and replaced with the more 'easily handled and rigorously defined notion of subjective health status'. Measures of subjective health are valuable in their own right since the outcomes being sought by most of those seeking health care are a reduction in symptoms and improvements in function, irrespective of their impact on overall life quality. 411

This is consistent with their view that quality of life is an 'idiosyncratic mystery'. It is also consistent with their view that the proper role of health care is the improvement of health status that is, health care is concerned with the removal of potential barriers to the quality of life rather than with the quality of life itself. For those who feel that the quality of life is a legitimate concern of health professionals and the health care system, the problem of how it can be measured remains. Two options mentioned above are the use of individualized measures or the fairly cumbersome approach suggested by Gill and Feinstein.412 Prudkin and Feinstein 411 suggest an alternative that acknowledges that an individual's health status can have a broader impact with respect to how they perceive themselves and their lives and allows this impact to be measured more simply..

This entails the use of subjective health status measures along with global ratings of quality of life and health-related quality of life; that is ratings of the extent to which quality of life is compromised by symptoms or functional and psychosocial problems. These ratings incorporate individuals' own beliefs, values and concerns and the relative importance of different life domains.

Consequently, they 'allow adequate expression of the way in which individual patients determine their own quality of life'. 411 They solve the problem of what existing measures actually measure, provide one way in which data on a unique, highly individualized phenomenon can be grouped for analysis, and provide a way of ascertaining the meaning of scores derived from instruments such as the Oral Health Impact Profile (OHIP), which have no intrinsic meaning. It is also consistent with the WHOQOL Group's approach. They argue that while data on functioning is important, global evaluations are the best indicators of quality of life.

The measures address the functional and psychosocial outcomes of oral disorders and can be readily used in population surveys or clinical trials. All document the frequency of impacts emanating from oral diseases that clinicians, investigators or research subjects have suggested are important. One of their main strengths is that they embody the notion that the patient's perspective has equal legitimacy to that of the clinician and should be taken into account when evaluating the consequences of disease and the outcomes of treatment for that disease. 410 The reviews of the five measures indicate that there is a degree of uncertainty with respect to both of these issues. None fully comply with the 'patient person-centred', 'importance' and 'validation' criteria for the development of measures which can be deemed to assess OH-QoL.

Adolescence is a period of life with specific health and developmental needs and rights. It is also a time to develop knowledge and skills, learn to manage emotions and relationships, and acquire attributes and abilities that will be important for enjoying the adolescent years and assuming adult roles.

All societies recognize that there is a difference between being a child and becoming an adult. How this transition from childhood to adulthood is defined and recognized differs between cultures and over time. In the past it has often been relatively rapid, and in some societies it still is. In many countries, however, this is changing. Linked to the hormonal and neurodevelopmental changes of adolescence are psychosocial and emotional changes and increasing cognitive and intellectual capacities.

Over the course of the second decade, adolescents develop stronger reasoning skills, logical and moral thinking, and become more capable of abstract thinking and making rational judgements. Changes in the adolescent's environment both affect and are affected by the internal changes of adolescence.

These external influences, which differ among cultures and societies, include social values and norms and the changing roles, responsibilities, relationships and expectations of this period of life. In many ways adolescent development drives the changes in the disease burden between childhood to adulthood. The appearance of certain health problems in adolescence, including substance use disorders, mental disorders and injuries, likely reflects both the biological changes of puberty and the social context in which young people are growing up.

Dental Caries, Fluorosis and Adolescent's Quality of Life

Dental caries is the commonest chronic disease of adolescence. The World Health Organization (WHO) has estimated that 60–90% of all adolescence are affected. 413,414 It was hypothesized that adolescence with greater dental caries experience would have higher impacts on their QoL, suggesting they are likely to have experienced more oral pain, had difficulties with chewing, have been worried or upset about their oral cavity or to have missed school due to their cumulative disease experience, 415 showing an indirect effect of clinical signs on daily functioning via reported symptom status, as predicted by Wilson and Cleary. 416

Further, despite low levels of dental caries and fluorosis, adolescence experienced appreciable impacts on OHRQoL. 417 These contradictory outcomes suggest that cultural norms and expectations influence adolescence's perception of their oral health and its effect on their QoL, as considered, as causal pathways between clinical variables may include individual and environment variables as both moderators and mediators. 416 In this way, studies of the relationship between the number of carious teeth and the OHRQoL are subject to criticism, as a result of the conceptual distinction between health and disease.

Consequently, although dental caries is relatively prevalent, it may not affect the adolescences ability to perform daily activities in its early stages. This implies that the relationship between OHRQoL and clinical indicators should be interpreted with caution, as the inconsistencies found in the relationships between clinical data and OHRQoL may not be due to the psychometric properties of the measures, but due to the fact that impacts are mediated by other factors.

All contemporary models of disease and its consequences, such as that of Wilson and Cleary,416 indicate that the relationships between biological variables and Health-Related Quality of Life (HRQoL) outcomes are not direct, but mediated by a variety or personal, social and environmental variables. In addition, it has been suggested that cultures and material deprivation can influence the extent of the impact of disease. 418

Variables such as general health status, household income and life stress have been shown to explain as much variance in the impact of oral disorders on adults as clinical indicators such as missing teeth. 419 Socioeconomic disparities in OHRQoL in a group of adolescence were found in Locker study. 425 That is, adolescents from low-income households had higher impacts on QoL than adolescence from high-income households, indicating poorer OHRQoL. .Further, household income remained a predictor of OHRQoL scores after controlling for the potential confounding effects of oral diseases and disorders such as dental caries, dental injury and malocclusion. A potential explanation may be differences in psychological assets and psychosocial resources.

Malocclusion and Adolescent's Quality of Life

Considering the categories of malocclusion severity, Foster Page et al. 415 observed a distinct gradient in the mean of emotional and social well-being domain scores, whereby those in the 'Handicapping' category had the highest scores and those in the 'Minor/ none' category had the lowest ones, on average. Similarly, O'Brien et al. 421 found statistically significant difference between the malocclusion and non-malocclusion groups only for the emotional and social well-being health domains.

Further, difficulty with smiling due to the position of teeth has been found to be one of the most important impacts of adolescence's OHRQoL. 422 These results suggest that the most significant impact of malocclusion on QoL is psychosocial, rather than conditions that influence oral health, such as oral or functional problems.

However, according to O'Brien et al., the Child Perceptions Questionnaire (CPQ) was not developed specifically to measure the impact of orthodontic problems and some of the questions in the functional and oral symptoms subscales are not necessarily relevant to patients with malocclusion. Nevertheless, Kok et al. 423 using different questions to test the construct validity of CPQ in adolescence, found the same results as the studies above 415,421 and only one study 424 found no relationship between malocclusion and QoL in adolescence.

This may reflect the difficulties that they may have with the concept of 'oral health' in relation to malocclusion. 425 These contradictory outcomes can be explained by the use of some OHRQoL measures in orthodontics, as is the Index of Orthodontics Treatment Need (IOTN) 426 which can emphasize malocclusion that may not be important to QoL, such as posterior cross bites. 424 Moreover, different meanings of QoL vary between and within individuals 420 according to culture and education, 427 contributing for distinct impacts of malocclusion on OHRQoL.

Gingival Problems and Adolescent's Quality of Life

Gum problems were the other important oral conditions affecting adolescent's OHRQoL, as shown by Gherunpong et al., 422 as more than one-fifth of adolescent's perceived that bleeding and swollen gums caused oral impacts on their life, particularly in relation to difficulty cleaning, a problem experienced by nearly half of all adolescent's. Moreover, who had difficulty with cleaning their teeth because of gum inflammation are unlikely to achieve good levels of oral hygiene, because brushing may lead to bleeding, and their gum problems would undoubtedly persist or even get worse.

It is apparent that sensitive teeth, toothache, oral ulcers were factors that contributed significantly to the incidence of impacts in adolescent children, and although this was high, the severity was not; many adolescents had their QoL affected at low levels. This reveals a need for further longitudinal studies to better understand and interpret OHRQoL measures in adolescents. Given the cross-sectional nature of the data studies, the observed findings addressed only the descriptive and discriminative potential of the OHRQoL measures in relation to adolescents' oral conditions.

The following explanations may account for the weak relationships found between OHRQoL and clinical data: there are low disease levels in the samples, the conditions under investigation may cause immeasurably low levels of impact or that impacts are mediated by a variety of factors such as culture and deprivation. 424 Although the observed prevalence of impacts was high in some studies, the severity was not; many adolescences had their QoL affected at low levels. 422,423 Furthermore, longitudinal studies need to be conducted to assess the evaluative properties of these OHRQoL measures.

What needs to be considered is that the way people feel about their QoL does not develop in isolation from their existing expectations (that constrain what is relevant) as well as the environment in which the margins of relevance are constructed, as the meaning of QoL changes over time. 420 Moreover, developmental changes unavoidably affect HRQoL of adolescence.

Maturity and an increase in age generate a more sophisticated understanding and perceptions about health and illness, 428 changing the perceptions about health and QoL in adolescence. 429 Difficulty with smiling was another important aspect of adolescents OHRQoL. It affected 40% of adolescents. The most prevalent cause was position of teeth.423 For example, de Oliveira and Sheiham found that adolescents with untreated malocclusions were significantly more likely to report oral impacts on their daily lives than those who had completed orthodontic treatment. Chen and Hunter found that psychological impacts of oral health, such as avoiding laughing and being teased about teeth, were more prevalent in adolescents than in adults and elderly. 430

FIFTEEN

Conclusion

To conclude with adolescent's oral health is often associated with socio-economic dimensions such as parental income and education.431,432 It was determined that family income, health insurance, and parental education level had a direct effect on adolescence's OHRQoL as well as indirectly affecting adolescence's oral health behaviour.

Many studies have reported a significant relationship between higher family income and better OHRQoL. 433,434 Previous studies focusing on adolescent have reported that different socio-economic conditions are related to the effect of oral diseases and disorders on OHRQoL, 435 but the magnitude of this effect is still controversial in pre-school adolescence.436

Wong et al 437 have shown that high family income has a protective effect on the OHRQoL of adolescent. It has been reported that family dental insurance and state financial support have a significant impact on OHRQoL. 438 Education is one of the primary methods of intercepting or preventing risky behaviours among adolescents.

It is important for health professionals to create awareness and understanding among their colleagues about some of the issues affecting these young adolescents, such as related injuries, unhealthful nutritional practices, substance abuse, and body art.

This knowledge can be passed along to patients who may be influenced in avoiding unnecessary risks and improve their health and safety. This information can be spread through heath educators or so-called teachers who can duly reach the adolescents in large scales at schools & colleges.

National level programs at schools should be insisted so as to bring about sense of awareness among the adolescent population. Also, enlightening parents would help most of the issues faced by adolescent be nurtured at an individual level, i.e.: direct one to one contact not making it awkward for the child. This shall also help them to be open about and discuss it with their parents or teachers.

Bibliography

1. Glick M, Williams DM, Kleinman DV, Vujicic M, Watt RG, Weyant RJ. A new definition for oral health developed by the FDI World Dental Federation opens the door to a universal definition of oral health. Br Dent J. 2016;221(12):792-793.

2. Sischo L, Broder HL. Oral health-related quality of life: what, why, how, and future implications. J Dent Res. 2011;90(11):1264-1270.

3. Rodd HD, Marshman Z, Porritt J, Bradbury J, Baker SR. Oral health-related quality of life of children in relation to dental appearance and educational transition. Br Dent J 2011; 211: E4.

4. Paula J, Leite I, Almeida A, Ambrosano G, Pereira A, Mialhe F. The influence of oral health conditions, socioeconomic status and home environment factors on schoolchildren's self-perception of quality of life. Health Qual Life Outcomes 2012; 10: 6.

5. Baker SR, Mat A, Robinson PG. What psychosocial factors influence adolescents' oral health? J Dent Res 2010; 89: 1230–1235.

6. Agou S, Locker D, Muirhead V, Tompson B, Streiner DL. Does psychological well-being influence oralhealth-related quality of life reports in children receiving orthodontic treatment? Am J Orthod Dentofacial Orthop 2011; 139: 369–377.

7. Chavers LS, Gilbert GH, Shelton BJ. Racial and socioeconomic disparities in oral disadvantage, a measure of oral health-related quality of life: 24-month incidence. J Public Health Dent 2002; 62: 140–147.

8. Foster Page LA, Thomson WM, Jokovic A, Locker D. Validation of the Child Perceptions Questionnaire (CPQ11–14). J Dent Res 2005; 84: 649–652.

9. Wong MCM, Lau AWH, Lam KF, McGrath C, Lu H-X. Assessing consistency in oral health-related quality of life (OHRQoL) across gender and stability of OHRQoL over time for adolescents using Structural Equation Modeling. Community Dent Oral Epidemiol 2011; 39: 325–335.

10. Newton JT, Corrigan M, Gibbons DE, Locker D. The self-assessed oral health status of individuals from White, Indian, Chinese and Black Caribbean communities in South-east England. Community Dent Oral Epidemiol 2003; 31: 192–199.

11. Locker D. Self-esteem and socioeconomic disparities in self-perceived oral health. J Public Health Dent 2009; 69:1 –8.

12. O'Brien K, Wright JL, Conboy F, Macfarlane T, Mandall N. The child perception questionnaire is valid for malocclusions in the United Kingdom. Am J Orthod Dentofacial Orthop 2006; 129: 536–540.

13. Do LG, Spencer A. Oral health-related quality of life of children by dental caries and fluorosis experience. J Public Health Dent 2007; 67: 132–139.

14. Traebert J, de Lacerda JT, Foster Page LA, Thomson WM, Bortoluzzi MC. Impact of traumatic dental injuries on the quality of life of schoolchildren. Dent Traumatol 2012;28:423–8.

15. Dame-Teixeira N, Alves LS, Ardenghi TM, Susin C, Maltz M. Traumatic dental injury with treatment needs negatively affects the quality of life of Brazilian schoolchildren. Int J Paediatr Dent 2013;23:266–73.

16. Marshman Z, Gibson BJ, Benson PE. Is the shortform Child Perceptions Questionnaire meaningful and relevant to children with malocclusion in the UK? J Orthod 2010; 37: 29 –36. [Erratum appears in J Orthod 2010;37:140].

17. Kiyak HA. Does orthodontic treatment affect patients' quality of life? J Dent Educ 2008; 72: 886–894.

18. Bernabe E, Sheiham A, De Oliveira CM. Impacts on daily performances attributed to malocclusions by British adolescents. J Oral Rehabil 2009; 36: 26– 31.

19. Park K. Park's Text Book of Preventive and Social Medicine. 19th ed. M/S Banarsidas Bhanot Publishers; 2007, Jabalapur, India.

20. Higginson IJ, Carr AJ. Measuring quality of life: Using quality of life measures in the clinical setting. BMJ 2001;322:1297-300.

21. Gift HC, Atchison KA, Dayton CM. Conceptualizing oral health and oral health-related quality of life. Soc Sci Med 1997;44:601-8.

22. DHHS Oral health in America: A report of the Surgeon General. Rockville, Maryl and: US Department of Health and Human Services, National Institute of Dental and Craniofacial Research, National Institute of Health; 2000. p. 7.

23. Sudaduang G, Tsakos G and Sheiham A. Developing and evaluating an oral health related quality of life index for children; Child-OIDP. CDH. 2004; 21:161-169.

24. Nucă C, Amariei C, Martoncsak E, Tomi D D. Study regarding the correlation between the Child-OIDP index and the dental status in 12-year-old children from Harsova, Constanta county. OHDMBSC. 2005; 4(4):04-13.

25. Barbosa T S and Gaviao M B. Oral health related quality of life in children: part I. How well do children know themselves? A systematic review. Int J Dent Hyg. 2008; 6: 93-99

26. Gift H C and Redford M. Oral health and the quality of life. Clin Geriatr Med. 1992; 8: 673-683.

27. Sheiham A. Theories explaining health behavior. In: Gjermo P,ed. Promotion of selfcare in oral health. A Symposium held in Oslo, Norway, September 10- 12; 1986:105-124.

28. Kleinman A. The illness narratives: Suffering, healing, and the human condition. Basic books; 2020 Oct 13.

29. Whoqol Group. The World Health Organization quality of life assessment (WHOQOL): position paper from the World Health Organization. Social science & medicine. 1995 Nov 1;41(10):1403-9.

30. Slade GD, Spencer AJ. Development and evaluation of the Oral Health Impact Profile. Community Dent Health. 1994 Mar;11(1):3-11.

31. Broder HL, Slade G, Caine R, Reisine S. Perceived impact of oral health conditions among minority adolescents. Journal of Public Health Dentistry. 2000 Sep;60(3):189-92.;

32. McGrath C, Bedi R. Measuring the Impact of Oral Health on Quality of Life in Britain Using OHQoL-UK©. Journal of public health dentistry. 2003 Jun;63(2):73-7.)

33. United States. Public Health Service. Office of the Surgeon General, National Institute of Dental, Craniofacial Research (US). Oral health in America: a report of the Surgeon General. US Public Health Service, Department of Health and Human Services; 2000

34. Broder HL, Wilson-Genderson M. Reliability and convergent and discriminant validity of the Child Oral Health Impact Profile (COHIP Child's version). Community dentistry and oral epidemiology. 2007 Aug;35:20-31.

35. Broder HL. Using psychological assessment and therapeutic strategies to enhance well-being. The Cleft palate-craniofacial journal. 2001 May;38(3):248-54.;

36. Strauss RP. "Only skin deep": health, resilience, and craniofacial care. The Cleft palate-craniofacial journal. 2001 May;38(3):226-30.

37. Lopez SJ, Snyder CR, Rasmussen HN. Striking a vital balance: Developing a complementary focus on human weakness and strength through positive psychological assessment.

38. Patrick DL, Edwards TC, Topolski TD. Adolescent quality of life, part II: initial validation of a new instrument. Journal of adolescence. 2002 Jun 1;25(3):287-300.

39. McGrath C, Bedi R. Measuring the Impact of Oral Health on Quality of Life in Britain Using OHQoL-UK©. Journal of public health dentistry. 2003 Jun;63(2):73-7.

40. Atchison KA, Dolan TA. Development of the geriatric oral health assessment index. Journal of dental education. 1990 Nov;54(11):680-7.

41. Fitzpatrick R, Davey C, Buxton MJ, Jones DR. Evaluating patient-based outcome measures for use in clinical trials. Health Technol Assess 1998; 2:1– 72.

42. Guyatt GD, Cook DJ. Health status, quality of life and the individual. JAMA 1994;272:630–1.

43. Leplege A, Hunt S. The problem of quality of life in medicine. JAMA 1997;278:47–50.

44. Locker D. An Introduction to Behavioural Science and Dentistry. London: Routledge; 1989.

45. Locker D. Concepts of oral health. Disease and the quality of life. In: Slade GD, editor. Measuring oral health and quality of life. Chapel Hill: University of North Carolina, Dental Ecology; 1997.

46. Locker D, Clarke M, Payne B. Self-perceived oral health status, psychological well-being and life satisfaction in an older adult population. J Dent Res 2000;79:970–5.

47. Locker D, Matear D, Stephens M, Jokovic A. Oral health-related quality of life of a population of medically compromised elderly people. Community Dent Health 2002;19:90–7.

48. Kressin NR. The Oral Health Related Quality of Life Measure (OHQOL). In: Slade GD, editor. Measuring oral health and quality of life. Chapel Hill: University of North Carolina, Dental Ecology; 1997. p. 114–9.

49. Albrecht GL, Devlieger PJ. The disability paradox: high quality of life against all odds. Soc Sci Med 1999;48:977–88.

50. Carr AJ, Higginson IJ. Are quality of life measures patient centred? Brit Med J 2001;322:1357–60.

51. Gill TM, Feinstein AR. A critical appraisal of the quality of quality-of-life measurements. JAMA 1994;272:619–26.

52. Adunuri NR, Feldman BM. Critical appraisal of studies measuring quality of life in juvenile idiopathic arthritis. Arthritis care & research. 2015 May;67(6):880-4.

53. Fitzpatrick R, Davey C, Buxton MJ, Jones DR. Evaluating patient-based outcome measures for use in clinical trials. Health Technol Assess 1998; 2:1– 72. BIBLIOGRAPHY 220

54. Guyatt GD, Cook DJ. Health status, quality of life and the individual. JAMA 1994;272:630–1.

55. Leplege A, Hunt S. The problem of quality of life in medicine. JAMA 1997;278:47–50.

56. Slade GD (ed). Measuring oral health and quality of life. Chapel Hill: University of North Carolina, Dental Ecology, 1997.

57. Djikers M. Measuring quality of life: methodological issues. J Phys Med Rehabil 1999. 78:286–300.

58. DeJong G. Value perspectives and the challenge of managed care. In: Fuhrer M, editor. Assessing Medical Rehabilitation Practice. Baltimore: Brookes Publishing Co.; 1997. p. 73–85.

59. Carr AJ, Higginson IJ. Are quality of life measures patient centred? Brit Med J 2001; 322:1357–60.

60. Frisch MB, Cornell J, Villanueva M, Retzlaff PJ. Clinical validation of the Quality of Life Inventory: A measure of life satisfaction for use in treatment planning and outcome assessment. Psychol Assess 1992;4:92–101.

61. Frisch MB. Self confidence in life test. Minneapolis, MN: MCS; 1994.

62. Bowling A. What things are important in people's live? A survey of the public's judgements to inform scales of health-related quality of life. Soc Sci Med 1995;41:1447–62.

63. Juniper EF, Guyatt GH, Jaeschcke R. How to develop and validate a new healthrelated quality of life instrument. In: Spiker B, editor. Quality of Life and Pharmacoeconomics in Clinical Trials. 2nd edn. Philadelphia: Raven Publishers, 1996. p.197–208.

64. Guyatt G, Bombardier C, Tugwell P. Measuring disease-specific quality of life in clinical trials. J Can Med Assoc 1986; 134:889–95.

65. Prutkin JM, Feinstein AR. Quality-of-life measurements: origin and pathogenesis. Yale J Biol Med 2002; 75:79–93.

66. Atchison KA, Dolan TA. Development of the Geriatric Oral Health Assessment Index. J Dent Educ 1990; 54:680–7.

67. Slade DG, Spencer AJ. Development and evaluation of the Oral Health Impact Profile. Community Dent Health 1994; 11:3–11.

68. Adulyanon S, Sheiham A. Oral impacts on daily performances. In: Slade GD, editor. Measuring oral health and quality of life. Chapel Hill: University of North Carolina, Dental Ecology; 1997. p. 152–60.

69. Jokovic A, Locker D, Stephens M, Kenny D, Tompson B. Validity and reliability of a measure of child oral health-related quality of life. J Dent Res 2002;81:459–63.

70. Cornell JE, Saunders MJ, Paunovich ED, Frisch MB. Oral Health Quality of Life Inventory (OH-QoL). In: Slade GD, editor. Measuring oral health and quality of life. Chapel Hill: University of North Carolina, Dental Ecology; 1997. p. 136–49.

71. Gift HC & Redford M. Oral health and the quality of life. Clin Geriatr Med 1992; 8: 673-83.

72. Reisine ST. (1981). Theoretical considerations in formulating sociodental indicators. Soc Sci Med; 745-50.

73. Badley EM. The ICIDH: format, application in different settings, and distinction between disability and handicap. A critique of papers on the application of the International Classification of Impairments, Disabilities, and Handicaps. Int Disabil Stud 1987; 9: 122-5.

74. Locker D. Measuring oral health: a conceptual framework. Community Dent Health 1988; 5: 3-18.

75. Heydecke G. Patie nt-based outcome measures: oral health-related quality of life. Schweiz Monatsschr Zahnmed 2002; 112: 605-11.

76. Inglehart MR & Bagramian RA. (2002). Oral Health-Related Quality of Life, Quintessence Publishing Co, Inc. John MT, Patrick DL, Slade JD. The German version of the Oral Health Impact Profile--translation and psychometric properties. Eur J Oral Sci; 2002; 110: 425-33.

77. Chen MS, Andersen RM, Barmes DE, Leclerq MH, Lyttle CS, World Health Organization. Comparing oral health care systems: a second international collaborative study. World Health Organization; 1997.

78. Slade G. Assessment of Oral HealthRelated Quality of Life. Oral Health-Related Quality of Life. 2002.

79. Guyatt G & Walter S. Measuring change over time: assessing the usefulness of evaluative instruments. J Chronic Dis 1987; 40: 171-8.

80. Chavers LS, Gilbert GH, Shelton BJ. Two-year incidence of oral disadvantage, a measure of oral health-related quality of life. Community Dent Oral Epidemiol 2003; 31: 21-9.

81. Allen PF. Assessment of oral health related quality of life. Health Qual Life Outcomes 2003; 1: 40.

82. Slade GD & Spencer AJ. Development and evaluation of the Oral Health Impact Profile. Community Dent Health 1994; 11: 3-11.

83. Jones JA. Using oral quality of life measures in geriatric dentistry. Community Dent Health 1998; 15: 13-8.

84. Allen PF, McMillan AS, Locker D. An assessment of sensitivity to change of the Oral Health Impact Profile in a clinical trial. Community Dent Oral Epidemiol 2001; 29: 175-82.

85. Awad MA, Lund JP, Dufresne E, Feine JS. Comparing the efficacy of mandibular implantretained overdentures and conventional dentures among middle-aged edentulous patients: satisfaction and functional assessment. Int J Prosthodont 2003a; 16: 117-22.

86. Allen F & Locker D. A modified short version of the oral health impact profile for assessing healthrelated quality of life in edentulous adults. Int J Prosthodont 2002; 15: 446-50.

87. Awad MA, Locker D, Korner-Bitensky N, Feine JS. Measuring the effect of intra-oral implant rehabilitation on health-related quality of life in a randomized controlled clinical trial. J Dent Res 2000; 79: 1659-63.

88. McGrath C, Alkhatib MN, Al-Munif M, Bedi R, Zaki AS. Translation and validation of an Arabic version of the UK oral health related quality of life measure (OHQoL-UK) in Syria, Egypt and Saudi Arabia. Community Dent Health 2003a; 20: 241-5.

89. Locker D & Allen PF. Developing short-form measures of oral health-related quality of life. J Public Health Dent 2002; 62: 13-20.

90. McGrath C, Hegarty AM, Hodgson TA, Porter SR. Patient-centred outcome measures for oral mucosal disease are sensitive to treatment. Int J Oral Maxillofac Surg 2003d; 32: 334-6.

91. Adulyanon S & Sheiham A. Oral impacts on daily performances. Measuring oral health and quality of life. G. Slade. Chapel Hill, University of North Carolina 1997.

92. Melas F, Marcenes W, Wright PS. Oral health impact on daily performance in patients with implant-stabilized overdentures and patients with conventional complete dentures. Int J Oral Maxillofac Implants 2001; 16: 700-12.

93. Tsakos G, Marcenes W, Sheiham A. Evaluation of a modified version of the index of Oral Impacts on Daily Performances (OIDP) in elderly populations in two European countries. Gerodontology 2001; 18: 121-30.

94. Masalu JR & Astrom AN. Social and behavioral correlates of oral quality of life studied among university students in Tanzania. Acta Odontol Scand 2002; 60: 353-9.

95. Masalu JR & Astrom AN. Applicability of an abbreviated version of the oral impacts on daily performances (OIDP) scale for use among Tanzanian students. Community Dent Oral Epidemiol 2003; 31: 7-14.

96. Astrom AN & Okullo I. Validity and reliability of the Oral Impacts on Daily Performance (OIDP) frequency scale: a cross-sectional study of adolescents in Uganda. BMC Oral Health 2003; 3: 5.

97. Robinson PG, Gibson B, Khan FA, Birnbaum W. Validity of two oral healthrelated quality of life measures. Community Dent Oral Epidemiol 2003; 31: 90- 9.

98. Locker D, Jokovic A, Clarke M. Assessing the responsiveness of measures of oral health-related quality of life. Community Dent Oral Epidemiology 2004; 32: 10-18.

99. Atchison KA & Dolan TA. Development of the Geriatric Oral Health Assessment Index. J Dent Educ 1990; 54: 680-7.

100. Dolan TA, Peek CW, Stuck AE, Beck JC. Threeyear changes in global oral health rating by elderly dentate adults. Community Dent Oral Epidemiol 1998; 26: 62-9.

101. Locker D. Issues in measuring change in selfperceived oral health status. Community Dentistry and Oral Epidemiology 1998; 26: 62-69.

102. Jokovic A, Locker D, Stephens M, Kenny D, Tompson B, Guyatt G. Validity and reliability of a questionnaire for measuring child oral-healthrelated quality of life. J Dent Res 2002; 81: 459-63.

103. Jokovic A, Locker D, Stephens M, Guyatt G. Agreement between mothers and children aged 11-14 years in rating child oral health-related quality of life. Community Dent Oral Epidemiol 2003a; 31: 335-43.

104. Cunningham SJ, Garratt AM, Hunt NP. Development of a conditionspecific quality of life measure for patients with dentofacial deformity: I. Reliability of the instrument. Community Dent Oral Epidemiol 2000; 28: 195- 201.

105. Slade DG, Spencer AJ. Development and evaluation of the Oral Health Impact Profile. Community Dent Health 1994;11:3–11.

106. Hunt SM, McEwan J, McKenna SP. Measuring health. London: Croom Helm; 1986

107. Carr AJ, Higginson IJ. Are quality of life measures patient centred? Brit Med J 2001;322:1357–60.

108. Locker D, Matear D, Stephens M, Jokovic A. Oral health-related quality of life of a population of medically compromised elderly people. Community Dent Health 2002;19:90–7.

109. Straus RP, Hunt RJ. Understanding the value of teeth to older adults. Influences on the quality of life. JADA 1993;124:105–10.

110. Gherunpong S, Tsakos G, Sheiham A. Developing and evaluating an oral health related quality of life index for children: The Child-OIDP. Community Dent Health 2004;21:161–9.

111. Atchison K. The General oral Health Assessment Index (The Geriatric Oral Health Assessment Index). In: Slade GD, editor. Measuring oral health and quality of life. Chapel Hill: University of North Carolina, Dental Ecology, 1997, p. 71–80.

112. Jokovic A, Locker D, Stephens M, Kenny D, Tompson B. Validity and reliability of a measure of child oral health-related quality of life. J Dent Res 2002;81:459–63

113. Locker D, Jokovic A, Stephens M, Kenny D, Tompson B, Guyatt G. Family impact of child oral and oro-facial conditions. Community dentistry and oral epidemiology. 2002 Dec;30(6):438-48.

114. Jokovic A, Locker D, Stephens M, Kenny D, Tompson B, Guyatt G. Measuring parental perceptions of child oral health-related quality of life. J Public Health Dent 2003;63:67–72.

115. Jokovic A, Locker D, Guyatt G. Development and evaluation of an oral health-related quality of life outcome measure for children 8 to 10 years old. Pediatric Dent 2004;26:512–8

116. Thomson WM, Foster Page LA, Gaynor WN, Malden PE. Short-form versions of the Parental-Caregivers Perceptions Questionnaire and the Family Impact Scale. Com- munity Dent Oral Epidemiol 2013; 41: 441–450.

117. Allison PJ, Locker D, Feine JS. Quality of life: a dynamic construct. Soc Sci Med. 1997;45:221–30.

118. C. G. Victora, S. R. Huttly, S. C. Fuchs, and M. T. A. Olinto, "The role of conceptual frameworks in epidemiological analysis: a hierarchical approach," International Journal of Epidemiology, vol. 26, no. 1, pp. 224–227, 1997.

119. Locker, D. Measuring Oral Health And Quality Of Life: Concepts Of Oral Health, Disease And Quality Of Life; University of North Carolina, Canada; 1997; 11-24.

120. Williams J, Wake M, Hesketh. Health–Related Quality of Life of Overweight and Obese Children. JAMA. 2005;293(1):70-6

121. Seid M, Varna JW, Segall D, Kurtin PS. Health-related quality of life as a predictor of pediatric healthcare costs: a two year prospective cohort analysis. Health and Quality of Life Outcomes. 2004, 2:48.

122. Wilson IB, Cleary PD. Linking clinical variables with health-related quality of life. A conceptual model of patient outcomes. JAMA 1995; 273: 59–65.

123. Sixou JL. How to make a link between Oral Health-Related Quality of Life and dentin hypersensitivity in the dental office?. Clinical oral investigations. 2013 Mar;17(1):41-4.

124. Sheiham A, Alexander D, Cohen L, Marinho V, Moysés S, Petersen PE, et al. Global Oral Health Inequalities: Task Group-Implementation and delivery of oral health strategies. Adv Dent Res. 2011May;23(2):259-67.

125. Lee, G. H., McGrath, C., Yiu, C. K., & King, N. M. (2010). A comparison of a generic and oral health-specific measure in assessing the impact of early childhood caries on quality of life. Community Dentistry and Oral Epidemiology, 38, 333–339.

126. Huntington NL, Spetter D, Jones JA, Rich SE, Garcia RI, Spiro III A. Development and validation of a measure of pediatric oral health-related quality of life: the POQL. Journal of public health dentistry. 2011 Jun;71(3):185-93.

127. Paula JS, Leite IC, Almeida AB, Ambrosano GM, Pereira AC, Mialhe FL. The influence of oral health conditions, socioeconomic status and home environment factors on schoolchildren's self-perception of quality of life. Health and quality of life outcomes. 2012 Dec;10(1):1-8.

128. Pradeep Kumar, Habib Ahmad Alvi, JitendraRao, BalendraPratap Singh, Sunit Ku- mar Jurel, Lakshya Kumar, Himanshi Aggarwal. Assessment of the quality of life in maxillectomy patients: A longitudinal study. J AdvProsthodont 2013;5:29-35

129. Andiappan M, Gao W, Bernabé E, Kandala NB, Donaldson AN. Malocclusion, orthodontic treatment, and the Oral Health Impact Profile (OHIP-14): Systematic review and meta-analysis. The Angle Orthodontist. 2015 May 1;85(3):493-500.

130. BATISTA, MariliaJesus, PERIANES, Lílian Berta Rihs, HILGERT, Juliana Balbinot, HUGO, Fernando Neves, & SOUSA, Maria da Luz Rosário de. (2014). The impacts of oral health on quality of life in working adults. Brazilian Oral Research, 28(1), 1-6. Epub August 26, 2014.

131. Sfreddo CS, Moreira CH, Nicolau B, Ortiz FR, Ardenghi TM. Socioeconomic inequalities in oral health-related quality of life in adolescents: a cohort study. Quality of Life Research. 2019 Sep 15;28(9):2491-500.

132. Sun, L., Wong, H.M. & McGrath, C.P.J. The factors that influence oral health-related quality of life in young adults. Health Qual Life Outcomes 16, 187 (2018).

133. Buldur B, Güvendi ON. Conceptual modelling of the factors affecting oral health-related quality of life in children: A path analysis. International Journal of Paediatric Dentistry. 2020 Mar;30(2):181-92.

134. World Health Organization. Orientation programme on adolescent health for health care providers.

135. The health of youth. WHO. Geneva, 1989 (document A42/Technical Discussions/2).

136. Berer M. By and for young women and men. Reproductive Health Matters, 2001,9(17) :6-9.

137. Tanner JM. Foetus into man: Physical growth from conception to maturity. Wells, Open Books Publishing Ltd, 1978.

138. Adapted from Hofmann AD, Greydanus DE, eds. Adolescent medicine. 2nd edition. Appleton and Lange, 1989.

139. Workgroup BF, Committee on Practice and Ambulatory Medicine. 2019 recommendations for preventive pediatric health care. Pediatrics. 2019 Mar 1;143(3).

140. Dean JA, editor. McDonald and Avery's Dentistry for the Child and Adolescent-E-book. Elsevier Health Sciences; 2015 Aug 10.

141. Yu-Jin Choi1,2 , Jung-Ok Choi1 Current Pediatric Research (2017) Volume 21, Issue 4The effects of the oral care behaviours of adolescents on self-perceived oral health

142. Rajesh G, Seemanthini S, Naik D, Pai K, Rao A. Disparities in Oral Health Behaviour among Young Adults in Mangalore, India: A Psychosocial Perspective. Journal of clinical and diagnostic

143. Silk H, Kwok A. Addressing adolescent oral health: a review. Pediatr Rev. 2017 Feb 1;38(2):61-8.

144. Sischo L, Broder HL. Oral health-related quality of life: what, why, how, and future implications. Journal of dental research. 2011 Nov;90(11):1264-70.

145. Viner RM, Ozer EM, Denny S, Marmot M, Resnick M, Fatusi A, Currie C. Adolescence and the social determinants of health. The lancet. 2012 Apr 28;379(9826):1641-52.

146. Choi YJ, Choi JO. The effects of the oral care behaviors of adolescents on self-perceived oral health. Curr Pediatric Res. 2017;21.

147. Psychosocial Behavioural Patterns for Adolescents Diana M. Gardiner, PhDa, *, Paul C. Armbruster, MS, DDSb

148. Macgregor ID, Regis D, Balding J. Self-concept and dental health behaviours in adolescents. J Clin Periodontol 1997;24(5):335–9.

149. O¨stberg A-L, Jarkman K, Lindblad U, et al. Adolescents' perceptions of oral health and influencing factors: a qualitative study. Acta Odontol Scand 2002;60(3):167–73.

150. Studen-Pavlovich D, Pinkham JR, Adair SM. The dynamics of change. In: Casamassimo PS, Fields HW Jr.McTigue DJ, Nowak AJ, eds. Pediatric Dentistry: Infancy Through Adolescence. 5th ed, St. Louis, Mo.: Elsevier Saunders; 2012:557-617.

151. Ajzen I. Attitudes, personality, and behavior. McGraw-Hill Education (UK); 2005 Nov 1.

152. Haustein S, Klöckner CA, Blöbaum A. Car use of young adults: The role of travel socialization. Transportation research part F: traffic psychology and behaviour. 2009 Mar 1;12(2):168-78.

153. Hrubes, D., Ajzen, I., and Daigle, J., 2001. Predicting hunting intentions and behaviour: An application of the theory of planned behaviour. Leisure Sciences, 23, 14.

154. Sparks B. Planning a wine tourism vacation? Factors that help to predict tourist behavioural intentions. Tourism management. 2007 Oct 1;28(5):1180- 92.

155. Arnett, J. J., 1998. Learning to stand alone: The contemporary american transition to adulthood in cultural and historical context. Human development, 41 (5-6), 295-315.

156. Fingerman, K. L., and Pitzer, L., 2007. Socializaion in old age. In: Grusec, J. E., and Hastings, P. D. eds. Handbook of socialization. New York: Guilford, 232-255.

157. Somerville LH, Sasse SF, Garrad MC, Drysdale AT, Abi Akar N, Insel C, Wilson RC. Charting the expansion of strategic exploratory behaviour during adolescence. Journal of experimental psychology: general. 2017 Feb;146(2):155.

158. Alexopoulos EC, Stathi IC, Charizani F. Prevalence of musculoskeletal disorders in dentists. BMC Musculoscelet International Journal of Applied Dental Sciences Disord. 2004; 5

159. Myers HL, Myers LB. 'It's difficult being a dentist': stress and health in the general dental practitioner. Br Dent J. 2004; 197(2):89-93.

160. Rising DV, Bennett BC, Hursh K, Plesh O. Reports of body pain in a dental student population. JADA 2005; 132:81-86.

161. Hollister MC, Anema MG. Health behavior models and oral health: a review. American Dental Hygienists' Association. 2004 Jun 1;78(3):6-.

162. Armitage CJ, conner M."THE HEALTH BELIEF MODEL"A Decade later"health education behaviour 1984;11;(1)1-47.

163. Hochbaum G. Health Behaviour. Belmont, CA: Wadsworth Publishing; 1970 70.

164. Studen-Pavlovich D, Pinkham JR, Adair SM. The dynamics of change. In: Casamassimo PS, Fields HW Jr.McTigue DJ, Nowak AJ, eds. Pediatric Dentistry: Infancy Through Adolescence. 5th ed, St. Louis, Mo.: Elsevier Saunders; 2012:557-617.

165. Harrison JA, Mullen PD, Green LW. A meta-analysis of studies of the health belief model with adults. Health education research. 1992 Mar 1;7(1):107-16.

166. Stokes E, Ashcroft A, Platt MJ. Determining Liverpool adolescents' beliefs and attitudes in relation to oral health. Health education research. 2005 Sep 28;21(2):192-205.

167. Hollister MC, Anema MG. Health behaviour models and oral health: a review. American Dental Hygienists' Association. 2004 Jun 1;78(3):6-.

168. Ajzen I, Fishbein M. Belief, Attitude, Intention, and Behaviour: An Introduction to Theory and Research, Addision-Wesley. Reading. 1975.

169. Tedesco LA, Keffer MA, Fleck-Kandath C. Self-efficacy, reasoned action, and oral health behaviour reports: a social cognitive approach to compliance. Journal of Behavioural Medicine. 1991 Aug 1;14(4):341-55.

170. Jönsson B, Baker SR, Lindberg P, Oscarson N, Öhrn K. Factors influencing oral hygiene behaviour and gingival outcomes 3 and 12 months after initial periodontal treatment: an exploratory test of an extended Theory of Reasoned Action. Journal of clinical periodontology. 2012 Feb;39(2):138-44.

171. Prochaska JO, Norcross JC, DiClemente CC. Changing for good. New York: Avon Books; 1994.

172. Prochaska JO, Velicer WF. The transtheoretical model of health behaviour change. American journal of health promotion. 1997 Sep;12(1):38- 48.

173. Tedesco LA, Keffer MA, Davis EL, Christersson LA. Effect of a social cognitive intervention on oral health status, behaviour reports, and cognitions. J Periodontol 1992;637:567-575.

174. Herzog TA, Abrams DB, Emmons KM, Linnan LA, Shadel WG. Do processes of change predict smoking stage movements? A prospective analysis of the transtheoretical model. Health Psychology. 1999 Jul;18(4):369.

175. Abdi J, Eftekhar H, Mahmoodi M, Shojaeizade D, Sadeghi R. Lifestyle of the employees working in Hamadan public sectors: application of the transtheoretical model. Iranian Red Crescent Medical Journal. 2015 Feb;17(2).

176. Bandura A. Self- efficacy: the exercise of control. New York: Freeman; 1997

177. Schunk DH. Self-efficacy and academic motivation. Educational psychologist. 1991 Jun 1;26(3-4):207-31.;

178. Bandura A. Social cognitive theory: An angentic perspective. Annu Rev Psychol 2001;52:1-26

179. Muris P. Relationships between self-efficacy and symptoms of anxiety disorders and depression in a normal adolescent sample. Personality and individual differences. 2002 Jan 19;32(2):337-48.

180. Lee JY, Divaris K, Baker AD, Rozier RG, Vann Jr WF. The relationship of oral health literacy and self-efficacy with oral health status and dental neglect. American journal of public health. 2012 May;102(5):923-9.

181. Syrjälä AM, Knuuttila ML, Syrjälä LK. Self-efficacy perceptions in oral health behaviour. Acta Odontologica Scandinavica. 2001 Jan 1;59(1):1-6.

182. Wallston KA, Stein MA, Smith CA. Form C of the MCHL scales: a condition specific measurement of locus of control. J Pers Assess 1994;633:534-553.

183. Reisine S, Litt M. Social and psychological theories and their use for dental practice. Int Dent J 1993;433Suppl 1:279-287

184. Regis D, Macgregor ID, Balding JW. Differential prediction of dental health behaviour by self-esteem and health locus of control in young adolescents. Journal of clinical periodontology. 1994 Jan;21(1):7-12.

185. Antonovsky A. Health stress and coping. San Francisco, CA: JosseyBass; 1979.

186. Freire MC, Hardy R, Sheiham A. Mothers' sense of coherence and their adolescent children's oral health status and behaviours. Community Dent Health 2002;191:24-31

187. Do Carmo Matias Freire M, Sheiham A, Hardy R. Adolescents' sense of coherence, oral health status, and oral health-related behaviours. Community dentistry and oral epidemiology. 2001 Jun;29(3):204-12.

188. Eriksson M, Lindström B. Antonovsky's sense of coherence scale and the relation with health: a systematic review. Journal of epidemiology & community health. 2006 May 1;60(5):376-81.

189. Savolainen J, Suominen-Taipale AL, Hausen H, Harju P, Uutela A, Martelin T, Knuuttila M. Sense of coherence as a determinant of the oral health- related quality of life: a national study in Finnish adults. European journal of oral sciences. 2005 Apr;113(2):121-7.

190. Elyasi M, Abreu LG, Badri P, Saltaji H, Flores-Mir C, Amin M. Impact of sense of coherence on oral health behaviours: a systematic review. PloS one. 2015 Aug 14;10(8):e0133918.

191. Ajzen, Icek (1991). "The theory of planned behaviour". Organizational Behaviour and Human Decision Processes. 50 (2): 179–211

192. Ajzen, I. (1989). Attitude structure and behaviour. Attitude structure and function, 241-274.

193. Guo Q, Johnson CA, Unger JB, Lee L, Xie B, Chou CP, Palmer PH, Sun P, Gallaher P, Pentz M. Utility of the theory of reasoned action and theory of planned behaviour for predicting Chinese adolescent smoking. Addictive behaviours. 2007 May 1;32(5):1066-81.

194. Fisher WA, Kohut T, Salisbury CM, Salvadori MI. Understanding human papillomavirus vaccination intentions: Comparative utility of the theory of reasoned action and the theory of planned behaviour in vaccine target age women and men. The journal of sexual medicine. 2013 Oct 1;10(10):2455-64.

195. Witkiewitz, K. & Marlatt, G.A. (2004). Relapse Prevention for Alcohol and Drug Problems. American Psychologist, 59, 4, 224-235.

196. "Relapse Prevention & Comeback". Ambrosia Treatment Center. Ambrosia Treatment Center. September 15, 2016. Retrieved June 7, 2017.

197. Stephens RS, Roffman RA, Simpson EE. Treating adult marijuana dependence: a test of the relapse prevention model. Journal of consulting and clinical psychology. 1994 Feb;62(1):92.

198. Schwarzer, R. (2008). Modeling health behaviour change: How to predict and modify the adoption and maintenance of health behaviours. Applied Psychology: An International Review, 57(1), 1–29.

199. Lippke, S., Ziegelmann, J. P., Schwarzer, R., & Velicer, W. F. (2009). Validity of stage assessment in the adoption and maintenance of physical activity and fruit and vegetable consumption. Health Psychology, 28, 183–193.

200. Sutton, S. (2005). Stage models of health behaviour. In M. Conner & P. Norman (Eds.), Predicting health behaviour: Research and practice with social cognition models (2nd ed., pp. 223–275). Maidenhead, England: Open University Press

201. Sniehotta, F. F., Scholz, U., & Schwarzer, R. (2006). Action plans and coping plans for physical exercise: A longitudinal intervention study in cardiac rehabilitation. British Journal of Health Psychology, 11, 23–37.

202. Luszczynska, A., Mazurkiewicz, M., Ziegelmann J. P., & Schwarzer, R. (2007). Recovery self-efficacy and intention as predictors of running or jogging behaviour: A cross-lagged panel analysis over a two-year period. Psychology of Sport and Exercise, 8, 247–260.

203. Radtke T, Scholz U, Keller R, Hornung R. Smoking is ok as long as I eat healthily: Compensatory Health Beliefs and their role for intentions and smoking within the Health Action Process Approach. Psychology & health. 2012 Oct 1;27(sup2):91-107.

204. Rogers, R. W. (1975). "A protection motivation theory of fear appeals and attitude change". Journal of Psychology. 91 (1): 93–114.

205. Pechmann, C; Goldberg, M; Reibling, E (2003). "What to convey in antismoking advertisements for adolescents: The Use of protection motivation theory to identify effective message themes". Journal of Marketing. 67 (2): 1– 18.

206. Maddux JE, Rogers RW. Protection motivation and self-efficacy: A revised theory of fear appeals and attitude change. Journal of experimental social psychology. 1983 Sep 1;19(5):469-79.

207. Dongre AR, Deshmukh PR, Boratne AV, Thaware P, Garg BS. An approach to hygiene education among rural Indian school going children. Online Journal of Health and Allied Sciences. 2008 Jan 24;6(4).

208. Phiri KS. Articles The prevalence, intensity and ecological determinants of helminth infection among children in an urban and rural community in Southern Malawi. Malawi Medical Journal. 2001;13(3):22-6.

209. Child Advocacy: Getting It Right for Children [Internet] available from https://residency.pediatrics.med.ufl.edu/files/2012/02/adolescent-hygienebasics.pdf accessed on 24/07/2020 at 12:30 PM

210. Kaur R, Kaur K, Kaur R. Menstrual hygiene, management, and waste disposal: practices and challenges faced by girls/women of developing countries. Journal of environmental and public health. 2018 Feb 20;2018.

211. Loe, H.: Meehanieal and chemical control of dental plaque. J. Clin. PeriodontoL 1979: 6: 32-36.

212. SuoMi, J. D.: Prevention and control of periodontal disease. Review of dental research. J, Am. Dent, Assoc. 1971: 83: 1271-1287.

213. Ainamo, J.: The effect of habitual tooth cleansing on the occurrence of periodontal disease and dental caries. Suotn. Hammaslaeaek. Toim. 1971: 67: 63-70.

214. linn, E. L.: What dental patients don't know about preventive care. J. Public Health Dent. 1974: 34: 39-41.

215. Petrovski: Yteinen psykotogia. Kansankulttuuri, Helsinki 1974.

216. Bibii'i, B. G.: Do we tell the truth about preventing caries? J. Dent. Child, 1966: 33: 269-279.

217. Axelsson, P., Lindhe, J. & Waseby, J.: The effect of various plaque control measures on gingivitis and caries in schoolchildren. Community Dent. Oral Epidemiol. 1976: 4: 232-239.

218. Finkelstein, P. & Grossman, E.: The effectiveness of dental floss in reducing gingival inflammation. J. Dent. Res. 1979: 58: 1034-1039.

219. Gjr.Rmo, P. & Flotra, L.: The effect of different methods of interdental cleaning. J. Periodontat Res, 1970: 5: 230

220. Wright, G. Z., Banting, D. W. & Feasby, W. H.: Effect of interdental flossing on the incidence of proximal caries in children. J Dental Research. 1977: 56.- 574-578

221. Terhune, J. A.: Predicting the readiness of elementary school children to learn an effective dental flossing technique. J. Am. Detit, Assoc, 1973: 86: 1332-1336.

222. Sutton, R. & Sheiham, A.: The factual basis of dental health education. A review. Health Educ. 7. 1974: 55.- 49-55.

223. Lang, N. P., Cumming, B. R. & Loe, H.: Toothbrushing frequency as it relates to plaque development and gingival health. J. Periodotitol. 1973: 44: 396-405.

224. Kriegsberg, L. &Treiman,B.R.: Preventive utilization of dentists' services among teenagers. J. Atn. Coll. Dent 1962: 29: 28-45.

225. Blinkhorn, A. S.: Influenee of soeiai norms on toothbrushing behavior of preschool children. Community Dent. Oral Epidemiol. 1978: 6: 222-226.

226. Kegeles, S. S.: Some motives for seeking preventive dental eare. J. Am. Dent, Assoc. 1963: 67: 90-98.

227. Murtomaa, H . & Ainamo, J.: Coneeptions of Finnish people about their periodontal situation. Community Dent. Oral Epidemiol 1977: 5; 195-199.

228. Richards, N. D.: Methods and effectiveness of health education. The past, present and future of social scientific involvement. Soc. Sci. Med, 1975: 9: 141-156.

229. Anderson JL: Integration of plaque control into the practice of dentistry. Dent Clin North Am 1972; 16:621

230. Charters WJ: Eliminating mouth infections with the toothbrush and other stimulating instruments. Dent Digest 1932; 38:130.

231. Fones AC: Mouth Hygiene, ed 4. Philadelphia, Lea & Febiger, 1934.

232. Leonard JF: Conservative treatment of periodontoclasia. J Am Dent Assoc 1939; 26:1308.

233. Bjorn H, Lindhe J: On the mechanics of toothbrushing. Odont Revy 1966; 17:9.

234. Gjermo P, Flotra L: The effect of different methods of interdental cleaning. J Periodont Res 1970; 5:230.

235. Goldman HM: The effect of single and multiple toothbrushing in the normal and periodontally involved dentition. Oral Surg 1956; 9:203.

236. Kinane DF: The role of interdental cleaning in effective plaque control: need for interdental cleaning in primary and secondary prevention. In: Proceedings of the Euro pean Workshop on Mechanical Plaque Control. Chicago, Quintessence, 1998

237. Third World Water Forum. Ministerial Declaration. 23 March 2003. Kyoto, Japan. http:/ /www.mofa.go.jp/ policy/ environment/wwf/declaration. html (6 July 2004).

238. World Health Organization. The World Health Report 2002: Reducing Risks, Promoting Healthy Life. Geneva: World Health Organization, 2002: xiii,68,129.

239. Pruss A, Kay D, Fewtrell L, Bartram J. Estimating the burden of disease from water, sanitation and hygiene at a global level. Environ Health Perspect 2002;110:537–42.

240. Esrey S, Potash J, Robert L, Shiff C. Effects of improved water supply and sanitation on ascariasis, diarrhea, dracunculiasis, hookworm infection, schistosomiasis and trachoma. Bull WHO 1991; 69:609-21.

241. Curtis V, Cairncross S. Effect of washing hands with soap on diarrhea risk in the community: a systematic review. The Lancet Infect Dis 2003; 3: 275– 81.

242. Rajab LD, Pertersen PE ,Bakaeen G, Hamdan MA. Oral health behaviour of schoolchildren and parents in Jordan. Int J Paediatric Dentistry 2002;12:168–76.

243. Huttly SRA, Morris SS, Pisani V. Prevention of diarrhea in young children in developing countries. Bull World Health Organ 1997; 75:165-74.

244. Taani DS. al-Wahadni AM, alOmari M. The effect of frequency of toothbrushing on oral health of 14-16 year olds. J Irish Dent Association 2003;49:15-20.

245. Borghi J, Guinness L, Quedrago J et al. Is hygiene promotion costeffective? A case study in Burkina Faso. Trop Med Int Health 2002; 7: 960–69.

246. Honkala E, Kannas L, Rimpela M, Wold B, Aaro E, Gilles P. Dental health habits in Austria, England, Finland and Norway. Int Dent J 1988;38:131- 38.

247. Honkala R, Kannas L, Rise J. Oral health habits of schoolchildren in 11 European countries. Int Dent J 1990;40:211-17.

248. Kuusela S, Honkala E, Kannas L, Tynjala J, Wold B. Oral hygiene habits of 11- year-old schoolchildren in 22 European Countries and Canada in 1993/1994. J Dent Res 1997;76:1602–609.

249. Kuusela S, Honkala E, Rimpela A, Karvonen S, Rimpela M. Trends in toothbrushing frequency among Finnish adolescents between 1977 and 1995. Community Dent Health 1997; 14:84– 88.

250. Macgregor IDM, Balding JW. Toothbrushing frequency and personal hygiene in 14-year-old schoolchildren. Dent Health 1988;27:12-5.

251. Macgregor IDM, Balding JW. Self-esteem as a predictor of toothbrushing behaviour in young adolescents. J Clin Periodontol 1991;18:312- 16.

252. Macgregor IDM, Regis D, Balding J. Self-concept and dental health behaviours in adolescents. J Clin Periodontol 1997;24:335-39.

253. Macgregor IDM, Balding JW. Toothbrushing frequency, cleanliness, and smoking habits in young adolescents. Clin Preventive Dentistry 1987; 9:18– 22.

254. Studen-Pavlovich D, Pinkham JR, Adair SM. The dynamics of change. In: Casamassimo PS, Fields HW Jr., McTigue DJ, Nowak AJ, eds. Pediatric Dentistry: Infancy Through Adolescence. 5th ed, St. Louis, Mo.: Elsevier Saunders; 2012:557-617.

255. National Institutes of Health. Consensus development conference statement: Diagnosis and management of dental caries throughout life, March 26-28, 2001. J Am Dent Assoc 2001;132(8):1153-61.

256. Baker SR, Mat A, Robinson PG. What psychosocial factors influence adolescents' oral health? J Dent Res 2010;89(11):1230-5.

257. Yu SM, Bellamy HA, Schwalberg RH, Drum MA. Factors associated with use of preventive dental and health services among U.S. adolescents. J Adolesc Health 2001;29(6):395-405.

258. Beltrán-Aguilar ED, Barker LK, Canto MT, et al. Surveillance for dental caries, dental sealants, tooth retention, edentulism, and enamel fluorosis— United States, 1988- 1994 and 1999-2002. MMWR Surveill Summ 2005;54(3):1-43.

259. Dye BA, Tan S, Smith V, et al. Trends in oral health status: United States, 1988-1994 and 1999-2004. National Center for Health Statistics. Centers for Disease Control and Prevention. U.S. Department of Health and Human Services, Hyattsville, Md. Vital Health Stat 2007;11(248):1-92. Available at: "http://www.cdc.gov/nchs/data/series/sr_11/sr11_248.pdf". Accessed September 2, 2015.

260. Kirkham J, Robinson C, Strong M, Shore RC. Effects of frequency of acid exposure on demineralization/remineralization behavior of human enamel in vitro. Caries Res 1994;28(1):9-13.

261. Howze KA. Health for Teens in Care: A Judge's Guide 2002. Washington, DC: American Bar Association; 2002.

262. Centers for Disease Control and Prevention. Recommendations for using fluoride to prevent and control dental caries in the United States. MMWR Recomm Rep 2001;50(RR14):1-42.

263. Weyant RJ, Tracy SL, Anselmo TT, et al. Topical fluoride for caries prevention: Executive summary of the updated clinical recommendations and supporting systematic review. J Am Dent Assoc 2013;144(11):1279-91.

264. American Academy of Pediatric Dentistry. Guideline on fluoride therapy. Pediatr Dent 2015;37(special issue):176-9.

265. Macgregor ID, Balding J, Regis D. Tooth-brushing schedule, motivation, and 'lifestyle' behaviours in 7,770 young adolescents. Community Dent Health 1996;13(4):232-7.

266. Dean JA, Hughes CV. Mechanical and chemotherapeutic home oral hygiene. In: Dean JA, Avery DR, McDonald RE, eds. McDonald and Avery's Dentistry for the Child and Adolescent. 9th ed. Maryland Heights, Mo.: Mosby Elsevier;

2011:205-22.

267. Freeman R, Sheiham A. Understanding decision-making process for sugar consumption in adolescents. Community Dent Oral Epidemiol 1997;25(3):228-32.

268. American Academy of Pediatric Dentistry. Policy on dietary recommendations for infants, children, and adolescents. Pediatr Dent 2015;37(special issue):56-8.

269. Feigal RJ. The use of pit and fissure sealants. Pediatr Dent 2002;24(5):415-22.

270. American Academy of Pediatric Dentistry. Guideline on restorative dentistry. Pediatr Dent 2015;37(special issue):232-43.

271. American Academy of Pediatric Dentistry. Guideline on prescribing dental radiographs for infants, children, adolescents, and persons with special health care needs. Pediatr Dent 2015;37(special issue):319-21.

272. Donly K. Pediatric Restorative Dentistry Consensus Conference April 15-16, 2002, San Antonio, Texas. Pediatr Dent 2002;24(5):374-6.

273. Keels MA, Tatakis DN. Periodontal disease in children: Associated systemic conditions. Literature review current through August 2015. Available at: "http://www.uptodate.com/contents/periodontal-disease-in-childrenassociated-systemic-conditions". Accessed September 2, 2015.

274. Beck JD, Arbes SI Jr. Epidemiology of gingival and periodontal disease. In: Newman MG, Taki HH, Klokkevold PR, Carranza FA, eds. Carranza's Clinical Periodontology. 10th ed. St. Louis, Mo: Saunders Elsevier; 2006:117- 9.

275. Wilson TG Jr, Kornman KS. Fundamentals of Periodontics. 2nd ed. Hanover Park, Ill.: Quintessence Publishing; 2003:196-7.

276. American Academy of Periodontology. Periodontal therapy. J Periodontol 2001;72(11):1624-8.

277. Richardson G, Russell KA. Congenitally missing maxillary incisors and orthodontic treatment considerations for the single tooth implant. J Can Dent Assoc 2001;67(1):25-8.

278. American Academy of Pediatric Dentistry. Guideline on management considerations for pediatric surgery and oral pathology. Pediatr Dent 2015;37(special issue):279-88.

279. American Academy of Orofacial Pain. General assessment of the orofacial pain patient. In: de Leeuw R de, Klasser GD, eds. Orofacial Pain: Guidelines for Assessment, Diagnosis, and Management. 5th ed. Chicago, Ill.: Quintessence Publishing Co. Inc.; 2013:25-46.

280. Behr M, Driemel O, Mertins V, et al. Concepts for the treatment of adolescent patients with missing teeth. Oral Maxillofac Surg 2008;12(2):49-60.

281. American Academy of Pediatric Dentistry. Guideline on management of the developing dentition and occlusion in pediatric dentistry. Pediatr Dent 2015;37(special issue):253-65.

282. Chaushu S, Sharabi S, Becker A. Dental morphologic characteristics of normal versus delayed developing dentitions with palatally displaced canines. Am J Orthod Dentofacial Orthop 2002;121(4):339-46.

283. Kurol J. Early treatment of tooth eruption disturbances. Am J Orthod Dentofacial Orthop 2002;121(6):588-91.

284. Gassner R, Bösch R, Tuli T, Emshoff R. Prevalence of dental trauma in 6,000 patients with facial injuries: Implications for prevention. Oral Surg Oral Med Oral Pathol Oral Radiol Endod 1999;87(1):27-33.

285. Tesini DA, Soporowski NJ. Epidemiology of orofacial sports-related injuries. Dent Clin North Am 2000;44(1):1-18.

286. Ranalli DN. A sports dentistry trauma control plan for children and adolescents. J Southeast Soc Pediatr Dent 2002;8:8-9.

287. Sarrett DC. Tooth whitening today. J Am Dent Assoc 2002;133(11):1535-8.

288. Donly KJ. The adolescent patient: Special whitening challenges. Compend Contin Educ Dent 2003;24(4A):390-6.

289. American Academy of Pediatric Dentistry. Policy on use of dental bleaching for child and adolescent patients. Pediatr Dent 2015;37(special issue):76-8.

290. Johnston LD, O'Malley PM, Bachman JG, Schulenberg JE. Monitoring the Future National Results on Adolescent Drug Use: Overview of Key Findings, 2013. Ann Arbor, Mich.: University of Michigan, Institute for Social Research, 2014.

291. U.S. Department of Health and Human Services. Preventing Tobacco Use Among Young People: A Report of the Surgeon General. Atlanta, Ga.: U.S. Department of Health and Human Services, Public Health Service, Centers for Disease Control and Prevention, National Center for Chronic Disease Prevention and Health Promotion, Office on Smoking and Health; 1994. Available at: "http://profiles.nlm.nih.gov/NN/B/C/L/Q". Accessed September 2, 2015.

292. American Dental Association. Summary of policy and recommendations regarding tobacco: 1964-present. ADA Resolution 1H-1992. In: ADA Transactions 1992. Chicago, Ill.: ADA; 1993:598.

293. American Academy of Pediatric Dentistry. Guideline on recordkeeping. Pediatr Dent 2015;37(special issue):307-14.

294. Christensen GJ. Oral care for patients with bulimia. J Am Dent Assoc 2002;133(12):1689-91.

295. Cortes MI, Marcenes W, Sheiham A. Impact of traumatic injuries to the permanent teeth on the oral healthrelated quality of life in 12- to 14-year-old children. Community Dent Oral Epidemiol 2002;30(3):193-8.

296. American Academy of Pediatric Dentistry. Policy on intraoral and perioral piercing. Pediatr Dent 2015;37(special issue):69-70.

297. Larson RW. Toward a psychology of positive youth development. Am Psychologist 2000;55(1):170-83.

298. Romito L, McDonald JL Jr. Nutritional considerations for the dental patient. In: Dean JA, Avery DR, McDonald RE, eds. McDonald and Avery's Dentistry for the Child and Adolescent. 9th ed. Maryland Heights, Mo.: Mosby Inc.; 2011:223-40.

299. American Academy of Pediatric Dentistry. Guideline on management of dental patients with special health care needs. Pediatr Dent 2015;37(special issue):166-71.

300. Cohen L K, Jago J D. Toward the formulation of sociodental indicators. Int J Health Serv 1976; 6: 681–98.

301. Aitchison K, Dolan T. Development of the geriatric oral health assessment index. J Dent Educ 1990; 54: 680–7.

302. Rosenberg D, Kaplan S, Senie R, Badner V. Relationships among dental functional status, clinical dental measures and generic health measures. J of Dent Educ 1988; 52: 653–657.

303. Cushing A M, Sheiham A, Maizels J. Developing sociodental indicators-the social impact of disease. Community Dent Health. 1986; 3: 3–17.

304. Petersen PE. The World Oral Health Report 2003: continuous improvement of oral health in the 21st century – the approach of the WHO Global Oral Health Programme. Community Dentistry and Oral Epidemiology 2003;32 Suppl 1:3-24.

305. Sheiham A, Watt R. The common risk factor approach: a rational basis for promoting oral health. Community Dentistry and Oral Epidemiology 2000;28:399-406.

306. Yee R, Sheiham A. The burden of restorative dental treatment for children in Third World countries. International Dental Journal 2002;52:7- 10.

307. Locker D. Concepts of oral health, disease and the quality of life. In: Slade GD, editor. Measuring oral health and quality of life. Chapel Hill: University of North Carolina, Dental Ecology; 1997, pp. 11-23.

308. Acs G, Lodolini G, Kaminski S, Cisneros GJ. Effect of nursing caries on body weight in a pediatric population. Pediatric Dentistry 1992;14:302- 5.

309. Gherunpong S, Tsakos G, Sheiham A. The prevalence and severity of oral impacts on daily performances in Thai primary school children. Health and Quality of Life Outcomes 2004;2:57. Available from: http://www.hqlo.com/content/ 2/1/57

310. Goes PSA, Watt RG, Hardy R, Sheiham A. The prevalence and severity of dental pain in 14–15- year-old Brazilian schoolchildren. Community Dental Health (submitted).

311. Gift HC, Reisine ST, Larach DC. The social impact of dental problems and visits. American Journal of Public Health 1992;82:1663-8.

312. Adulyanon S, Vourapukjaru J, Sheiham A. Oral impacts affecting daily performance in a low disease Thai population. Community Dentistry and Oral Epidemiology 1996;24:385-9.

313. Sheiham A, Steele J. Does the condition of the mouth and teeth affect the ability to eat certain foods, nutrients, and dietary intake, and nutritional status amongst older people? Public Health Nutrition 2001;4:797-803.

314. Applewhite, H. L.: "Total Dental Care for the Adolescent," NY State Dent J, 40:83-87, 1974.

315. Casamassimo PS, Pinkham JR, Steinke D. Dental health needs of the adolescent. Pediatr Dent. 1979 Jun 1;1(2):129-37.

316. Aggeryd T. Goals for oral health in the year 2000: cooperation between WHO, FDI and the national dental associations. International dental journal. 1983 Mar 1;33(1):55-9.

317. Massler, M.: "Teenage Caries," Dent Clin North Am, 13:405- 424, 1969.

318. Kelly, J. E., and Harvey, C. R.: "Decayed, Missing and Filled Teeth Among Youths 12-17 Years," Vital and Health Statistics: Data from the National Health Survey, Series 1 I, No. 144, DHEW Publication No. (HRA) 75- 1626, 1974.

319. Greenberg, J. S.: "An Analysis of Various Teaching Modes in Dental Health Education," J Sch Health, 47:26-32, 1977.

320. Dunning, J. M.: "Chair-Time Needed for Dental Maintenance Care of Children at Different Ages," J Mass Dent Soc, 8:16-20, 1959

321. Suomi, J. D.: "Occurrence of Dental Caries Among Children and Youths in the United States," J Prev Dent, 5:20-23, 1978.

322. Brunswick, A. F., and Nikias, M.: "Dentist's Rating and Adolescents' Perceptions of Oral Health," J Dent Res, 54:836-843, 1975.

323. Linn, E. L.: "Teenager's Attitudes, Knowledge and Behaviours Related to Oral Health," J Am Dent Assoc, 92:946-951, 1976.

324. Baer, P. N. and Benjamin, S. D.: Periodontal Disease in Children and Adolescents, Philadelphia: J. B. Lippincott Co., 1974.

325. Sutcliffe, P.: "A Longitudinal Study of Gingivitis and Puberty," J Periodont Res, 7:52-58, 1972, 326. Ross CB. Oral health status and tradition in New Zealand. International Dental Journal. 1984 Dec 1;34(4):266-70.

327. Hicks MJ, Flaitz CM. Epidemiology of dental caries in the pediatric and adolescent population: a review of past and current trends. The Journal of clinical pediatric dentistry. 1993 Jan 1;18(1):43-9.

328. Biazevic MG, Rissotto RR, Michel-Crosato E, Mendes LA, Mendes MO. Relationship between oral health and its impact on quality of life among adolescents. Brazilian oral research. 2008 Mar;22(1):36-42.

329. Mashoto KO, Astrom AN, Skeie MS, Masalu JR. Socio-demographic disparity in oral health among the poor: a cross sectional study of early adolescents in Kilwa district, Tanzania. BMC Oral health. 2010 Dec 1;10(1):7.

330. Krisdapong S, Prasertsom P, Rattanarangsima K, Sheiham A. Sociodemographic differences in oral health-related quality of life related to dental caries in thai school children. Community Dent Health. 2013 Jun 1;30(2):112-8.

331. Chakravathy KP, Thippeswamy HM, Kumar N, Chenna D. Relationship of body mass index and dental caries with oral health related quality of life among adolescents of Udupi district, South India. European Archives of Paediatric Dentistry. 2013 Jun 1;14(3):155-9.

332. Lee MO, Lee EJ. Effects of adolescent and Oral health-related characteristics on dental caries. The Korean Journal of Health Service Management. 2018;12(2):101-12.

333. Bekes K, John MT, Schaller HG, Hirsch C. The German version of the child perceptions questionnaire on oral health-related quality of life (CPQ-G11- 14): population-based norm values. J Orofac Orthop. 2011;72:223-233.

334. Cadenas de Llano-Pérula M, Ricse E, Fieuws S, Willems G, Orellana-Valvekens MF. Malocclusion, Dental Caries and Oral Health-Related Quality of Life: A Comparison between Adolescent School Children in Urban and Rural Regions in Peru. International Journal of Environmental Research and Public Health. 2020 Jan;17(6):2038.

335. Das D, Misra J, Mitra M, Bhattacharya B, Bagchi A. Prevalence of dental caries and treatment needs in children in coastal areas of West Bengal. Contemporary clinical dentistry. 2013 Oct;4(4):482.

336. Dash JK, Sahoo PK, Bhuyan SK, Sahoo S. Prevalence of dental caries and treatment needs among children of Cuttack (Orissa). Journal-Indian society of Pedodontics and preventive dentistry. 2002 Dec 1;20(4):139-43.

337. De Oliveira CM, Sheiham A. Orthodontic treatment and its impact on oral health-related quality of life in Brazilian adolescents. Journal of orthodontics. 2004 Mar;31(1):20-7.

338. Bernabé E, Sheiham A, de Oliveira CM. Impacts on Daily Performances Related to Wearing Orthodontic Appliances: A Study on Brazilian Adolescents. The Angle Orthodontist. 2008 May;78(3):482-6.

339. Chen M, Wang DW, Wu LP. Fixed orthodontic appliance therapy and its impact on oral health-related quality of life in Chinese patients. The Angle Orthodontist. 2010 Jan;80(1):49-53.

340. Navabi N, Farnudi H, Rafiei H, Arashlow MT. Orthodontic treatment and the oral health-related quality of life of patients. Journal of Dentistry (Tehran, Iran). 2012;9(3):247.

341. Feu D, Miguel JA, Celeste RK, Oliveira BH. Effect of orthodontic treatment on oral health–related quality of life. The Angle Orthodontist. 2013 Sep;83(5):892-8.

342. Shaw WC, Richmond S, Kenealy PM, Kingdon A, Worthington H. A 20-year cohort study of health gain from orthodontic treatment. Am J Orthod. 2007;132:146–157.

343. Costa AA, Serra-Negra JM, Bendo CB, Pordeus IA, Paiva SM. Impact of wearing fixed orthodontic appliances on quality of life among adolescents: Case-control study. The Angle Orthodontist. 2016 Jan;86(1):121-6.

344. Mary AV, Mahendra J, John J, Moses J, Ebenezar AR, Kesavan R. Assessing quality of life using the oral health impact profile (OHIP-14) in subjects with and without orthodontic treatment need in chennai, tamil nadu, India. Journal of clinical and diagnostic research: JCDR. 2017 Aug;11(8):ZC78.

345. Anthony SN, Zimba K, Subramanian B. Impact of malocclusions on the oral health-related quality of life of early adolescents in Ndola, Zambia. International journal of dentistry. 2018 Jun 3;2018.

346. R. D. Castro, M. C. Portela, A. T. Leão, and M. T. de Vasconcellos, "Oral health-related quality of life of 11- and 12-year-old public school children in Rio de Janeiro," Community Dentistry and Oral Epidemiology, vol. 39, no. 4, pp. 336–344, 2011.

347. Grath CM, Bedi R, Gilthorpe MS. Oral health related quality of life-- views of the public in the United Kingdom. Community dental health. 2000 Mar;17(1):3-7.

348. Krisdapong S, Sheiham A, Tsakos G. Oral health-related quality of life of 12-and 15-year-old Thai children: findings from a national survey. Community dentistry and oral epidemiology. 2009 Dec;37(6):509-17.

349. Mbawalla HS, Masalu JR, Astrom AN. Socio-demographic and behavioural correlates of oral hygiene status and oral health related quality of life, the Limpopo-Arusha school health project (LASH): A cross-sectional study. BMC pediatrics. 2010 Dec 1;10(1):87.

350. Krisdapong S, Prasertsom P, Rattanarangsima K, Adulyanon S, Sheiham A. Setting oral health goals that include oral health-related quality of life measures: a study carried out among adolescents in Thailand. Cadernos de saude publica.2012;28:1881-92.

351. Usha GV, Thippeswamy HM, Nagesh L. Comparative assessment of validity and reliability of the Oral Impacts on Daily Performance (OIDP) frequency scale: a cross-sectional survey among adolescents in Davanagere city, Karnataka, India. International journal of dental hygiene. 2013 Feb;11(1):28-34.

352. Gupta E, Robinson P, Marya C, Baker S. Oral health inequalities: relationships between environmental and individual factors. J Dent Res. 2015;94(10):1362–8.

353. Keles S, Abacigil F, Adana F. Oral health status and oral health related quality of life in adolescent workers. Clujul Medical. 2018 Oct;91(4):462.

354. El-Kalla IH, Shalan HM, Bakr RA. Impact of dental trauma on quality of life among 11–14 years schoolchildren. Contemp Clin Dent. 2017;8(4):538– 544.

355. Soares JP, Barasuol JC, Torres FM, Giacomin A, Gonçalves BM, Klein D, et al. The impact of crown fracture in the permanent dentition on children's quality of life. Dent Traumatol. 2018;34(3):158–163.

356. Laganà G, Fabi F, Abazi Y, Kerçi A, Jokici M, Nastasi EB, Vinjolli F, Cozza P. Caries prevalence in a 7- to 15-year-old Albanian schoolchildren population. Ann Stomatol. 2012;3(2):38–43.

357. Thelen DS, Bårdsen A, Åstrom A. Applicability of an Albanian version of the OIDP in an adolescent population. Int J Paediatr Dent. 2011;21:289–298. doi: 10.1111/j.1365-263X.2011.01122.x.

358. Peter E, Baiju RM, Sreela LS, Varghese NO, Varughese JM. Does socioeconomic status and family type influence oral health-related quality of life in individuals with malocclusion?. Journal of Indian Orthodontic Society. 2018 Jun;52(2):89-93.

359. Sanadhya S, Aapaliya P, Jain S, Sharma N, Choudhary G, Dobaria N. Assessment and comparison of clinical dental status and its impact on oral health-related quality of life among rural and urban adults of Udaipur, India: A

cross-sectional study. Journal of basic and clinical pharmacy. 2015 Mar;6(2):50.

360. Sinha N, Shankar D, Vaibhav V, Vyas T, Singh A, Parihar AS. Oral health-related quality of life in children and adolescents of Indian Population. J Pharm Bioall Sci 2020;12, Suppl S1:619-22

361. Azodo, C.C., Agbor, A.M. Gingival health and oral hygiene practices of schoolchildren in the North West Region of Cameroon. BMC Res Notes 8, 385 (2015).

362. Elias-Boneta AR, Ramirez K, Rivas-Tumanyan S, Murillo M, Toro MJ. Prevalence of gingivitis and calculus in 12-year-old Puerto Ricans: a cross-sectional study. BMC oral health. 2018 Dec 1;18(1):13.

363. Gökalp S, Guciz Dogan B, Tekçiçek M, Berberoglu A, Ünlüer Ş. National survey of oral health status of children and adults in Turkey. Community Dental Health. 2010 Mar 1;27(1):12.

364. López R, Baelum V. Oral health impact of periodontal diseases in adolescents. Journal of dental research. 2007 Nov;86(11):1105-9.

365. Bisegger C, Cloetta B, Von Bisegger U, Abel T, Ravens-Sieberer U. Health-related quality of life: gender differences in childhood and adolescence. Sozial-und Präventivmedizin. 2005 Oct 1;50(5):281-91.

366. Ahuja N, Ahuja N. Influence of socioeconomic status and home environmental factors on oral health-related quality of life among school children in north Bengaluru, India: A cross-sectional study. Journal of Indian Association of Public Health Dentistry. 2017 Jul 1;15(3):220.

367. Locker D. Disparities in oral health-related quality of life in a population of Canadian children. Community Dent Oral Epidemiol 2007;35:348-56

368. Maria da rocha Kozmhinsky V, Heimer M, Goes P. Sociodemographic factors and oral health conditions related to the impact on the quality of life of adolescents. Pesquisa Brasileira em Odontopediatria e Clínica Integrada. 2016 Mar 20;16(1):35-42.

369. Mohamed S, Vettore MV. Oral clinical status and oral health-related quality of life: is socioeconomic position a mediator or a moderator?. International dental journal. 2019 Apr;69(2):119-29.

370. Sfreddo CS, Moreira CH, Nicolau B, Ortiz FR, Ardenghi TM. Socioeconomic inequalities in oral health-related quality of life in adolescents: a cohort study. Quality of Life Research. 2019 Sep 15;28(9):2491-500.

371. Eid SA, Khattab NM, Elheeny AA. Untreated dental caries prevalence and impact on the quality of life among 11 to14-year-old Egyptian schoolchildren: a cross-sectional study. BMC Oral Health. 2020 Dec;20(1):1-1.

372. Halfon N, Hochstein M. Life course health development: an integrated framework for developing health, policy and research. Milbank Q 2002;80(3):1–31.

373. Parcel GS, Nader PR, Meyer MP. Adolescent health concerns, problems, and patterns of utilization in a triethnic urban population. Pediatrics. 1977 Aug 1;60(2):157-64.

374. Schamschula RG, Cooper MH, Wright MC, Agus HM, Un PS. Oral health of adolescent and adult Australian Aborigines. Community dentistry and oral epidemiology. 1980 Oct;8(7):370-4..

375. Freire MD, Hardy R, Sheiham A. Mothers' sense of coherence and their adolescent children's oral health status and behaviours. Community dental health. 2002 Mar 1;19(1):24-31.

376. Bachman JG, Johnston LD, O'Malley PM. Smoking, drinking, and drug use among American high school students: correlates and trends, 1975-1979. American Journal of Public Health. 1981 Jan;71(1):59-69.

377. Spencer AJ. Trends in dental caries: Australian adolescents. Australian dental journal. 1986 Aug;31(4):262-7.

378. Benotsch EG, Snipes DJ, Martin AM, Bull SS. Sexting, substance use, and sexual risk behavior in young adults. Journal of adolescent health. 2013 Mar 1;52(3):307-13. 379. Honkala E, Kannas L, Rise J. Oral health habits of schoolchildren in 11 European countries. International Dental Journal. 1990 Aug 1;40(4):211-7.

380. Clerehugh V, Lennon MA, Worthington HV. 5-year results of a longitudinal study of early periodontitis in 14-to 19-year-old adolescents. Journal of Clinical Periodontology. 1990 Nov;17(10):702-8.

381. Vehkalahti M, Helminen S, Rytömaa I. Caries decline from 1976 to 1986 among 15-year-olds in Helsinki. Caries research. 1990;24(4):279-85.

382. Fitzgerald RP, Thomson WM, Schafer CT, Loose MA. An exploratory qualitative study of Otago adolescents' views of oral health and oral health care. The New Zealand dental journal. 2004 Sep 1;100(3):62-71.

383. Hollowell WH, Childers NK. A new threat to adolescent oral health: The grill. Pediatric dentistry. 2007 Jul 1;29(4):320-2.

384. Peres KG, Peres MA, Araujo CL, Menezes AM, Hallal PC. Social and dental status along the life course and oral health impacts in adolescents: a population-based birth cohort. Health and Quality of Life Outcomes. 2009 Dec 1;7(1):95.

385. Ostberg AL, Ericsson JS, Wennström JL, Abrahamsson KH. Socio-economic and lifestyle factors in relation to priority of dental care in a Swedish adolescent population. Swedish dental journal. 2010;34(2):87-94.

386. Ericsson JS, Östberg AL, Wennström JL, Abrahamsson KH. Oral health-related perceptions, attitudes, and behavior in relation to oral hygiene conditions in an adolescent population. European journal of oral sciences. 2012 Aug;120(4):335-41.

387. Maida CA, Marcus M, Hays RD, Coulter ID, Ramos-Gomez F, Lee SY, McClory PS, Van LV, Wang Y, Shen J, Cai L. Child and adolescent perceptions of oral health over the life course. Quality of Life Research. 2015 Nov 1;24(11):2739-51.

388. Allen MS, Robson DA, Martin LJ, Laborde S. Systematic review and meta-analysis of self-serving attribution biases in the competitive context of organized sport. Personality and Social Psychology Bulletin. 2020 Jul;46(7):1027-43.

389. Anand N, Suresh M, Chandrasekaran SC. Effect of obesity and lifestyle on the oral health of pre-adolescent children. Journal of clinical and diagnostic research: JCDR. 2014 Feb;8(2):196.

390. Smoking Control Strategies in Developing Countries. Technical Report Series 695. Geneva, World Health Organization, 1983.

391. Public Health Service: Teenage Smoking: National Patterns of Cigarette Smoking, Ages 12 Through 18, in 1972 and 1974. DHHS publication No. (NIH) 76-931. Government Printing Office, 1976.

392. Kandel DB, Yamaguchi K: Developmental Patterns of the Use of Legal, Illegal, and Medically Prescribed Psychotrophic Drugs from Adolescence to Young Adulthood. National Institute on Drug Abuse, research monograph 56. Government Printing Office, 1987.

393. McKennel AD, Thomas RK: Adults and Adolescents' Smoking Habits and Attitudes. Government Social Survey. London, Her Majesty's Stationery Office, 1969

394. Greenberg MA, Wiggins CL, Kutvirt DM, Samet JM: Cigarette use among Hispanic and non-Hispanic white school children, Albuquerque, New Mexico. Am J Public Health 1987; 77:621-622

395. Pederson LL, Lefcoe NM: Short- and long-term prediction of selfreported cigarette smoking in a cohort of late adolescents: Report of an 8- year follow-up of public school students. Prev Med 1987; 16:432-447.

396. Newcomb MD, Maddahian E, Bentler PM: Risk factors for drug use among adolescents: Concurrent and longitudinal analysis. Am J Public Health 1986; 76:525-531.

397. Mittelmark MB, Murray DM, Luepker RV, et al: Predicting experimentation with cigarettes: The childhood antecedents of smoking study (CASS). Am J Public Health 1987; 77:206-208 9.

398. Severson HE, Lichtenstein E: Smoking prevention programs for adolescents: Rationale and review. In Krasnegor NA, Arasten JD, Caraldo MF (eds): Child Health Behavior: A Behavioral Pediatric Perspective. New York, John Wiley & Sons, 1986, pp 281-309.

399. Burk, W., Steglich, C., & Snijders, T. (2007). Beyond dyadic interdependence: Actor-oriented models for co-evolving social networks and individual behaviors. International Journal of Behavioral Development, 31, 397–404.

400. Umberson, D., & Montez, J. (2010). Social relationships and health: A flashpoint for health policy. Journal of Health and Social Behavior, 51, S54– S66.

401. Steinberg, L., & Monahan, K. (2007). Age differences in resistance to peer influenceDevelopmental. Psychology, 43, 1531–1543

402. Bronfenbrenner, U., & Morris, P. (2006). The bioecological model of human development. In R. M. Lerner & W. Damon (Eds.), The handbook of child psychology: Vol 1. Theoretical models of human development (5th ed., pp. 793–828). New York: Wiley.

403. Simons-Morton, B., & Farhat, T. (2010). Recent findings on peer group influences on adolescent substance use. The Journal of Primary Prevention, 31, 191–208.

404. Green, H., Horta, M., de la Haye, M., Tucker, J., Kennedy, D., & Pollard, M. (2013). Peer influence and selection processes in adolescent smoking behavior: A comparative study. Journal of Nicotine & Tobacco Research, 15, 534–541.

405. Eisenberg, M., Toumbourou, J., Catalano, R., & Hemphill, S. (2014). Social norms in the development of adolescent substance use: A longitudinal analysis of the international youth development study. Journal of Youth and Adolescence, 43, 1486–1497.

406. Cummings, K., & Proctor, R. (2014). The changing public image of smoking in the United States: 1964–2014. Cancer Epidemiology, Biomarkers & Prevention, 23, 32–36.

407. Brown, A., Moodie, C., Hastings, G., Mackintosh, A., Hassan, L., & Thrasher, J. (2010). The association of normative perceptions with adolescent smoking intentions. Journal of Adolescence, 33, 603– 614.

408. WHOQOL Group. The World Health Organization quality of life assessment (WHOQOL): Position paper from the World Health Organization. Soc Sci Med 1995; 41:1403–9. BIBLIOGRAPHY 262.

409. Fitzpatrick R, Davey C, Buxton MJ, Jones DR. Evaluating patient-based outcome measures for use in clinical trials. Health Technol Assess 1998; 2:1– 72.

410. Leplege A, Hunt S. The problem of quality of life in medicine. JAMA 1997; 278:47–50. 411. Prutkin JM, Feinstein AR. Quality-of-life measurements: origin and pathogenesis. Yale J Biol Med 2002; 75:79–93.

412. Gill TM, Feinstein AR. A critical appraisal of the quality of quality-oflife measurements. JAMA 1994; 272:619–26.

413. World Health Organization. WHO Oral Health Data Bank. Geneva, World Health Organization, 2002.

414. World Health Organization. WHO Oral Health Country / Area Profile. Available at: http://www.whocollab.od.mah.se/index.html.

415. Foster Page LA, Thomson WM, Jokovic A, Locker D. Validation of the Child Perceptions Questionnaire (CPQ 11-14). J Dent Res 2005; 84: 649–652.

416. Wilson IB, Cleary PD. Linking clinical variables with healthrelated quality of life. A conceptual model of patient outcomes. J Am Med Assoc 1995; 273: 59–65.

417. Robinson PG, Nalweyiso N, Busingye J, Whitworth J. Subjective impacts of dental caries and fluorosis in rural Ugandan children. Community Dent Health 2005; 22: 231–236.

418. Wong AT, McMillan AS, McGrath C. Oral health-related quality of life and severe hypodontia. J Oral Rehabil 2006; 33: 869–873.

419. Locker D, Slade G. Association between clinical and subjective indicators of oral health status in an older adult population. Gerodontology 1994; 11: 108–114.

420. Gregory J, Gibson B, Robinson PG. Variation and change in the meaning of oral health related quality of life: a 'grounded' systems approach. Soc Sci Med 2005; 60: 1859–1868.

421. O'Brien C, Benson PE, Marshman Z. Evaluation of a quality of life measure for children with malocclusion. J Orthod 2007; 34: 185–193.

422. Gherunpong S, Tsakos G, Sheiham A. The prevalence and severity of oral impacts on daily performances in Thai primary school children. Health Qual Life Outcomes 2004; 12: 57.

423. Kok YV, Mageson P, Harradine NW, Sprod AJ. Comparing a quality of life measure and the Aesthetic Component of the Index of Orthodontic Treatment Need (IOTN) in assessing orthodontic treatment need and concern. J Orthod 2004; 31: 312–318.

424. Marshman Z, Rodd H, Stern M et al. An evaluation of the Child Perceptions Questionnaire in the UK. Community Dent Health 2005; 22: 151– 155.

425. Locker D. Disparities in oral health-related quality of life in a population of Canadian children. Community Dent Health 2007; 35: 348– 356.

426. Brook PH, Shaw WC. Development of an index of orthodontic treatment priority. Eur J Orthod 1989; 11: 309–320.

427. Lattanzi AP, Silveira FM, Guimarães L, Antunes LA, dos Santos Antunes L, Assaf AV. Effects of oral health promotion programmes on adolescents' oral health-related quality of life: A systematic review. International journal of dental hygiene. 2020 Aug;18(3):228-37.

428. Drotar D. Measuring health-related quality of life in children and adolescents: implications for research and practice. Mahwah, NJ, Lawrence Erlbaum Associates, 1998.

429. Wallander JL, Schmitt M, Koot HM. Quality of life measurement in children and adolescents: issues, instruments, and applications. J Clin Psychol 2001; 57: 571–585.edc e

430. Chen MS, Hunter P: Oral health and quality of life in New Zealand: a social perspective. Soc Sci Med 1996, 43:1213-1222

431. Abanto J, Carvalho TS, Mendes FM, Wanderley MT, Bönecker M, Raggio DP. Impact of oral diseases and disorders on oral health-related quality of life of preschool children. Community Dent Oral Epidemiol. 2011; 39:105-114.

432. Chaffee BW, Rodrigues PH, Kramer PF, Vítolo MR, Feldens CA. Oral health-related quality-of-life scores differ by socioeconomic status and caries experience. Community Dent Oral Epidemiol. 2017; 45:216-224.

433. Merdad L, El-Housseiny AA. Do children's previous dental experience and fear affect their perceived oral health-related quality of life (ohrqol)? BMC Oral Health. 2017; 17:47-56

434. Kumar S, Goyal A, Tadakamadla J, Tibdewal H, Duraiswamy P, Kulkarni S. Oral health related quality of life among children with parents and those with no parents. Community Dent Health. 2011; 28:227-231.

435. Paula JS, Leite IC, Almeida AB, Ambrosano GM, Pereira AC, Mialhe FL. The influence of oral health conditions, socioeconomic status and home environment factors on schoolchildren's self-perception of quality of life. Health Qual Life Outcomes. 2012; 10:1-6.

436. Schuch HS, dos Santos CF, Torriani DD, Demarco FF, Goettems ML. Oral health-related quality of life of schoolchildren: impact of clinical and psychosocial variables. Int J Paediatr Dent. 2015; 25:358-365.

437. Wong H, McGrath C, King N, Lo E. Oral health-related quality of life in Hong Kong preschool children. Caries Res. 2011; 45:370-376. 438. Locker D. Disparities in oral health-related quality of life in a population of Canadian children. Community Dent Oral Epidemiol. 2007; 35:348-356

Printed by Libri Plureos GmbH in Hamburg,
Germany